LOOKING AT THE CROSS

LOOKING AT THE CROSS

BRIAN HAYMES

First published 1988
International Bible Reading Association
Robert Denholm House
Nutfield, Redhill, Surrey RH1 4HW

British Library Cataloguing in Publication Data
Haymes, Brian
   Looking at the Cross
   1. Bible. N.T. Gospels. Special subjects: Jesus Christ.
   Passion – Expositions
   I. Title   II. National Christian Education Council
   232.9'6

ISBN 0–7197–0575–4

Cover design by Jan Gleaves

Typeset by Avonset, Midsomer Norton, Bath, Avon
Printed and bound by Cox and Wyman Ltd, Reading

To my Mother and Father

CONTENTS

Preface

I am grateful to the Revd Simon Oxley, General Secretary of the National Christian Education Council, who suggested that I might write this book, and to Joy Standen, the IBRA Editor, for her careful work on the manuscript.

Much of the manuscript was drafted while on study leave in Canada where the home of the Jackson family proved to be a special place to reflect on the love the cross inspires. My wife Jenny and I will never forget their kindness.

This book is not intended to be an academic study. Those who would like to explore further the detailed questions that narratives of the cross raise, might usefully consult *Passion Narratives of the Synoptic Gospels* by Herman Hendrickx (Geoffrey Chapman) and *The Cross: Tradition and Interpretation* by Hans-Reudi Weber (SPCK).

I am grateful to Jenny who typed the manuscript and helped with many encouraging conversations.

Brian Haymes
September 1987

1
By way of introduction

The cross of Jesus is at the centre of Christian faith and life. Each of the four Gospel writers focus their story on the last few days and hours of Jesus' life on earth and give attention to the cross out of all proportion to the rest of his life. That in itself shows how important they believed the cross to be. This book is concerned with what the Gospels of Matthew, Mark, Luke and John say about the crucifixion of Jesus. It is primarily a Bible study.

Why do Christian people pay so much attention to the Bible? Basically because in it is the foundation-story of our faith. The Bible is inspiring and authoritative. It tells us about God, and includes what Jesus said and did, and what happened to him and his followers. Through the Bible we receive guidance and encouragement for our present adventure of Christian discipleship. Mostly we read the Bible for these very practical reasons. We know we need to be Bible readers if we are to live as Christians, that is, as those whose lives are shaped by the Lord Jesus Christ and not simply by the fashions of the day. The history of the Church is a witness to the Bible's power to inspire, rebuke, correct and sustain Christians in all kinds of circumstances in their following of Jesus.

Neither we, nor the Bible, exists in a vacuum. For example, we might be in a village or inner city slum, in an area of famine or the affluent west, in a position of privilege or without power. People the world over read the Bible out of very different backgrounds. Every generation comes to the Bible out of its own social context. We bring with us issues and problems particular to our generation and we listen to the Scriptures because this major resource is needful if we are to make Christian decisions and take Christlike action. Even with the Bible in hand there is enough temptation for us to make of God and Jesus what suits us best. We can easily allow the world to squeeze us into its own mould (from Romans 12.2, J. B. Phillips' translation). Without constantly listening to the basic story in the Bible that temptation is a trap into which we shall almost certainly fall. In this book, therefore, we shall look at the story of the cross as it is variously told in the Gospels so that we may grow in our knowledge of Jesus and be guided and strengthened for our discipleship today.

Three different churches

Before I came to teach at a theological college I had been the minister of three different Baptist churches. In each of these the Christian Year was carefully observed as we marked and celebrated the festivals of the faith. By doing this we kept ourselves in touch with the whole story that Christians tell of God's ways with us and especially as they find crucial focus in Jesus.

So, like many congregations, we prepared for Christ's coming in the four Sundays of Advent, leading to Christmas praise and celebration. Then we marked Christ's baptism. His temptations were recalled at the start of Lent and carefully we followed his way to the cross, taking Holy Week a day at a time.

For the purposes of this book we are going to pause at the cross. The story goes on, of course, to the triumph of Easter, Ascension, the giving of the Spirit at

Pentecost and even further; but we are concentrating on the cross of Jesus.

Each of the three churches kept Good Friday as a special day. Geographically, they were miles apart and local customs, sacred and secular, meant that Good Friday was acknowledged in very different ways. In one place all of the shops, factories and offices closed, no one went to work, although not everyone came to worship. In another, there was nothing outwardly special about the day at all and work went on as usual as it did on any other Friday. One consequence of all this was that the churches had to think hard about how best they could 'keep' Good Friday both as an act of witness to their neighbours and as a means of helping the members live and grow in the faith. It was a question both of recalling and proclaiming the cross. Let me describe what we did.

The first church was located on the growing edge of a big city. Not so many years previously it had been a village and it still kept some of the closeness that goes with village life. There was a genuine sense of community and shared identity and the various churches were well used to working together. On the edge of the community was some high open ground that fell quickly away to a river flanked by the local mills. From the top of this rise, which used to be a rubbish tip, there was a fine view over part of the industrial sector of the city and its new housing estates.

Early on Good Friday morning three large crosses were erected on the top of the hill, each about ten feet high. They stood there, with nails protruding from the wood. At the appointed hour, we walked silently from our homes to the crosses on the hill. There we read the Bible passages for the day, sang some hymns, heard an address on the meaning of the death of Jesus and prayed together for the world and the Church. Then, just as silently, we went home. The crosses remained looking out over the city. Many of us came back later, alone, to stand and pray and remember. It was a bleak, isolated place, literally on the edge, with the city's life open to view below us. The setting prompted all kinds of thoughts about the meaning and significance of the cross. It was our way of keeping Good Friday in that place.

The second church was in the middle of a much smaller city; only a large town really, but it served as the centre for a mainly rural region. As a result, it had hospitals, banks and offices out of all proportion to the precise needs of those who lived in the city. During our time there the central churches increasingly grew together in their sense of purpose and mission as, in different ways, we sought to affirm the presence of the living Christ in the city and to live out his kingdom.

Our years there also coincided with a time of social change as increasingly the new, big stores opened their doors for trade and the Good Friday life of the city altered. Previously shops and offices had closed for the day and the individual churches each held morning and afternoon services attended by their members. The social change led the churches to a new pattern. We all gathered in one of the church buildings for shared worship and then we processed through the city, stopping at various significant places making them our contemporary 'stations of the cross'. We paused outside the hospital, the city hall, in the new shopping complex and outside the lawcourts. We carried a large cross and wherever we stopped we read part of the Good Friday story and prayed together, remembering especially the people and their work in the building which was that particular 'station'. We were not protesting at Good

Friday trade, as some people including the media immediately thought, but we were publicly witnessing and proclaiming to the city something of the meaning of the cross for all our life. Then the whole company moved to another church for the traditional three hours of worship and meditation.

The third church was in a large city, built just within the 'inner ring'. There was no tradition here of the city recognising Good Friday as a day free from work because, as long as anyone could remember, it was a normal working day. Once again the central churches, or most of them, worked together. At the start of the day a large cross was set up in the city square. As many people from the churches as were able gathered there for a brief service which was mainly readings from the Gospel story. Then, for the rest of the day until the late evening, various congregations took responsibility for standing vigil at the cross. Some groups simply stood in silence, others read the Scriptures and sang songs, occasionally there would be some street theatre or mime. There was a tradition in the city, acknowledged by many of the businesses, which allowed employees who so wished to take an hour on Good Friday 'for religious purposes'. This meant that around the cross were people in business suits, overalls, or uniforms, remembering during their working hours God's work for the saving of the world.

The cross was set symbolically in the centre of that city's life. The majority of the inhabitants hardly noticed, or hurried by. Sometimes those of us who had kept vigil talked afterwards about the sense and relevance of what we had done. In one sense the gesture seemed so futile. Yet, it was heavy with meaning for a few of us, while seemingly being incomprehensible for the many. Perhaps the cross has always been like that.

In all these three contexts the same story was being told but in each place it was different; and every year the event was experienced differently by the same people. Any congregation can listen to the story of the cross together but it will be 'heard' in quite different ways by the individual members.

Three young people

This difference of experience is so, even in a close-knit group like a family. I talked about the cross with three of the children of the family mentioned in the *Preface*. They told me what they particularly saw in the passion story and what the cross meant to them.

Sarah, the youngest aged fifteen, said that she was always struck by the cruelty and pain of it all but that, somehow, God was involved and so it was very important. Becky spoke about God taking the pain, the sin, which caused the cross. She saw the cross as a place of hope and forgiveness because it was all about costly love, God's love for us and everyone. Their brother, Nat, was less than comfortable with any ideas of a stern and judgemental God because the cross gave him the strong sense that God is on our side. The cross spoke positively to him of the God who doesn't hassle us but who challenges us.

These responses express what the three young people 'saw' in the cross at the time I talked with them. They all said the story was very important but obviously they were responding in different ways. I am sure that a conversation with them a year later would show how they had come to 'see' even more in the cross of Jesus. Three children from a different kind of family would make other points.

There is nothing odd about Sarah, Becky and Nat responding in the way they did. From the first, people have been struck by the cross, in all manner of ways. Different truths have been perceived. Visions of glory and grief, victor and victim, rejection and acceptance, judgement and mercy, all these and more have been discerned in the message of the cross. The liturgies, the worship services of the churches, the hymns and prayers, all underline this great diversity of perception and understanding. Indeed, some people have been so moved and touched by the story of Good Friday that, for them, the cross is beyond words. To attempt to explain it, they say, would be to trivialise it, like when you attempt to put into words just how much you love someone. The poets get near to it but we more prosaic mortals are usually defeated.

Every generation of the Church sees different depths of meaning in the dying of Jesus. There is no one view that is total, final and ultimate. Part of the power of the story of the cross is its ability to touch, provoke, console, disturb, encourage, liberate and inspire people in this variety of ways. It always has been like that. Our eyes are fixed on one central point, but we all see differently. What we are given to see is not identical at all.

This phenomenon of seeing the same thing differently is there in the New Testament. The story of Jesus' death on the cross is told by all four Gospel writers and, basically, they all tell the same story; but not in the same way. It is obvious that this part of the story of Jesus has their special attention – nothing else in his life is described in such detail as the cross. Certainly this incident meant a great deal to them. But what did it mean? Each of the four tells the story in their own way. The accounts are different. There are details in one not recalled in the others. Emphases are made in

17

the telling which are by no means common to them all. We need to ask why this is.

What is a Gospel?

To attempt an answer we must travel by way of some other questions, such as, what kind of a document is a Gospel? Suppose you are a librarian classifying and cataloguing new books. There in the pile is *The Gospel* by Mark. Where would you put it on the library shelves? Is it history, biography, theology, fact or fiction? If it is meant to be a biography then we must say it is a very poor effort since it tells us so little about its subject. If it is meant to be a history book, again it does not seem to have been carefully written; and yet, there is enough historical detail to suggest that the whole thing is not a work of fiction. The person at the centre of the story appears to be historical enough, even if some very non-historical things are said about him. So where will you classify Mark's Gospel?

I think you will have to create an extra category called 'Gospel' because this work is a new kind of writing. Many New Testament scholars suggest that no one individual – say Mark, Matthew, Luke or John – stands as the sole and only author of these works but rather they come out of the experience of local congregations or groups of Christians who remembered and tried to live out the story of Jesus. There was a gap in time between the life, death and resurrection of Jesus and the writing down of the first Gospel. In that time the story of Jesus, what he did and taught, what happened to him and what he did for others, was remembered and retold, and obviously the different stories had all manner of effects in various contexts. It was the same story but its meaning could not be limited to one perception only. From the first, the cross spoke to people in different ways.

This recalling and retelling of the essential story would have gone on particularly when Christians gathered for worship – different congregations with various needs, reflecting their social, political, economic and religious contexts. It was in worship and in teaching that the all-important story was told and retold and so from the different communities there came the different Gospels. We would not be far wrong if we were to say that in listening to the Gospels today we are hearing the preaching and teaching of the church in Palestine, or Ephesus or Rome, or wherever the Gospels came from. This underlines the claim that the Gospels are unique as literature, indeed the title 'Gospel' was probably only given to these strange, fascinating and crucial works around AD 150. The churches remembered and celebrated the story of Jesus but not in the same way.

The purpose of this book

The purpose of this book is to look at the four Gospel accounts of the death of Jesus. Why are there differences in the four narratives and what kind of differences are they? Perhaps they are there because special factors in the group's situation made particular features of the story especially significant to them in their circumstances, struggling to live the Christian life as they understood it.

The Gospels are not dead documents, ancient works of long-lost writers who shut themselves away simply to write. They are committed works, written out of the heart of early Christian struggles to make sense of what God had done in the life, death and resurrection of Jesus. The Gospels were written as proclamation, encouragement and teaching. They are living records that sprang from an interaction between the Jesus story and the living issues that story provoked for the first Christians.

They tell the story differently because their situations are different. For example, the questions and issues that confront a largely Gentile church in a Gentile environment are not necessarily the same as those before a Jewish church in Palestine. Just think of the way the context affects the concerns and work of a church in the inner city compared with a church in a rural or suburban environment.

So, in the next four chapters, we shall look carefully at each of the Gospel accounts of the death of Jesus. We shall see how the Gospels tell the one story, but notice particularly the 'touches', the omissions and additions of each narrative. All four Gospel writers are theologians. They each have a particular perspective when it comes to understanding what God has done in Jesus. These perspectives relate to:

● The basic story of the crucifixion of Jesus which they had received.

● The context in which the congregation is living out its life – for example, a hostile environment or a welcoming society.

● The particular issues before that congregation as they looked for answers in the Gospel story. Sometimes the issues were raised within the culture and naturally the church turned to the story of Jesus as they worked out their response. At other times it was the story of Jesus that prompted practical issues of everyday life for them.

This is not to say that the Gospel writers accommodated the story of Jesus to fit the needs of the congregation. Rather, it was a proper pastoral concern that led them to realise that some parts of the story of Jesus were more significant in their context than others. Have you ever asked yourself why the stories remembered about Jesus are so selective? Why do we know so little about some parts of his life? Part of the answer is that what we would like to know now was not judged by the early Church to be as necessary and helpful as other, more essential, matters. The selection of stories, which we believe was made under the guidance of the Holy Spirit, was for evangelistic, pastoral and teaching purposes.

When we come to look at the four accounts of the crucifixion we shall try to see why some things are especially remembered and said in the way that they are. We shall attempt, so far as it is possible, to ground the story in the lives of the congregations. This will be the spring-board for us to ask in what way the story of the death of Jesus raises issues for today and in what way the challenges present in our attempts to live as Christians are lit up by the story of the cross.

There are at least two dangers before us in this enterprise. One is to take the Bible story as a direct, detailed instruction for all travellers, like the *Highway Code*. This attitude is tempting and is often found in people who have a high regard for Scripture and its teaching. But, within the New Testament itself, we shall see that Christians make different responses to the same Jesus. Christianity is a living faith and not just dull obedience to an old textbook. The other danger is in sitting so loose to the Bible story that we create the way of life we can manage, a life all-too-easily shaped not by the Gospel story but by the pressures of our own culture.

This, in summary, is how we shall proceed:

● First, we shall take note of the situation out of which each Gospel came. This is not an easy thing to do because we know so little about these situations and we must beware of going far beyond the evidence.

● Then we shall look closely at the Gospel story itself, noting especially where the life situation of the early Church is reflected in the story. We shall see this in the places where the Gospels record or omit different incidents or sayings.

● After that we shall summarise the main themes, especially as they relate to the understanding of the death of Jesus and the meaning of discipleship. Only then shall we try to bring these Gospel emphases and some of our present issues of discipleship together.

A suggestion

The hope of this book is that we should, through the Scriptures, grow in our knowledge and love of Christ, and so the primary task is to read the Bible. I suggest that at the start of each chapter you read the whole story of the cross in Mark, or whatever Gospel is our concern in that chapter. It will not take you long, but it will give you a feel for what the writer of the Gospel is saying.

Then you will see that the story has been broken up into shorter sections. Again, it is vital that you read that part of the Bible before turning to the comments made upon it.

You are probably reading this book on your own. At the end of each chapter there are some questions and suggestions for discussion. These are designed both to stimulate your own thought or to help a small group in its study.

The interaction of text and life is what we seek. Bringing both text and reader alive is the work of the Holy Spirit. So prayer is the appropriate way to begin our study together.

A prayer

O living God, you have kept your people following in the path of Jesus. When we have wandered, patiently you have redirected us and set us again on the way. May we, who look at the story of the cross, realise that it is planted firmly on our earth, so that with quiet trust we may learn of Jesus and follow the living Christ in the way he appoints and in the strength he supplies. Amen.

Some questions and suggestions for further thought

1 Try to recall the most memorable Good Friday in your life. What happened? Why do you think it is so memorable?

2 How does your own church spend Good Friday? Begin to think of what you might do next Holy Week.

3 What does the cross say to you now? Try to put into words what its significance is for your life.

2
Mark's story of the cross

It is generally believed today that Mark is the first of the Gospels to be written. It used to be thought that this was the bare uninterpreted story of Jesus, simply told. Now we realise that Mark too is a theologian, much concerned with the significance of the death of Jesus and Christian discipleship.

What do we know about the background of the congregation out of which this Gospel came? In hard undisputable terms, very little. The Gospel was possibly written from the city of Rome sometime between AD 64 and 75. In AD 64 Nero launched his persecution in which Christian leaders and church members are said to have died. The Gospel seems to have been addressed to Christians who knew, or expected to know, pain and suffering because they were disciples of Jesus. Here was early persecution for the faith. It also seems as though the Church was troubled by false Christs who would lead the Church astray. So there were tensions within and beyond the Church.

A strong tradition names John Mark as the author and that he recorded the reminiscences of Peter. More confidently we can say that the Church was largely made up of Gentile members. Certainly Mark is concerned with the Gentile mission of the early Church at a time of high expectation that the End of all things was at hand. The persecutions heightened that anticipation. Try to imagine a small minority group, of highly religious committed people, with deep hopes on which they had staked everything, now facing shame, suffering and death because of their loyalty to Jesus Christ. Let us now look at Mark's story.

The betrayal and arrest   Mark 14.43 – 52

Jesus is in the garden of Gethsemane with some sleepy disciples. He has had his own inward struggles but now rouses his friends to tell them that the betrayer is at hand.

Judas is the betrayer. Mark repeats what he has said before, that Judas is one of the twelve (14.10). The traitor is not an unknown anonymous enemy but a friend. He approaches with a crowd who are armed. They have come from the authorities.

Mark seems to underline the approach of Judas. The kiss of greeting between a disciple and a rabbi was common enough but what is more noteworthy is the complete absence of resistance by Jesus. He takes no steps to avoid what is happening. There is a reaction from an unidentified person who stands by but no response from Jesus.

He challenges the manner of his arrest. After all, Jesus has done nothing in secret. In daylight he has given his teaching. But now it is dark and they have come to arrest him as if he were a criminal. He is a teacher. He is innocent of any crime. Why then this arrest? And the answer is, 'let the scriptures be fulfilled' (14.49). It was the belief of the early Christians that Jesus' passion happened in accordance with Scripture, that is, it is the will of God. This divine necessity has been recognised in the passion predictions in Mark's Gospel (8.31; 9.31; 10.33 – 34). That is why Jesus is not to resist what is happening to him; neither are his friends.

But these friends are already on the run (verse 50). We ought to note that the word 'disciple' is not used between 14.32 and 16.7, between Gethsemane and the resurrection. Jesus is alone, isolated. Enemies are against him, and friends have forsaken him, and before him lies an even deeper forsakenness. Ever since he left the table and went into the garden he is on his own. Crowds surround him but he is isolated, marked out by God and man.

Verses 51 – 52 are curious. It has been suggested that this is John Mark's way of saying, 'I was there.' It certainly seems to stress the presence of an eyewitness, perhaps one of the crowd who later became a church member. But it is all very speculative.

Already four themes are identifiable:

● Jesus is a teacher. He is innocent of criminal charges. There is no earthly reason why anyone should treat him as a dangerous criminal.

● What is happening has heavenly reason. It is according to Scripture. It is the will of God.

● Jesus is isolated and alone, a solitary victim. There are no human resources coming to save him.

● These things, as recorded, actually happened. There can be no doubt that Jesus suffered. There are eyewitnesses.

Before the Sanhedrin   Mark 14.53 – 65

Jesus is taken for trial before all the chief priests, elders and scribes. Mark stresses that the whole Sanhedrin, the Jewish Council, was present (although it was night and the calling of the court would be irregular). This section reads as if everything is 'set up', except that the witnesses are totally disorganised! Mark says that they were already looking to put Jesus to death (verse 55), but it is quite clear that there is no evidence against him. A reading of the whole of Mark's Gospel gives the impression of gathering and increasing opposition to Jesus. This antagonism is now sharply in focus.

Mark describes a scene in which the Jewish leaders are presented as those who are really against Jesus. In this he probably reflects an early Church response which sought to lay blame on the Jews for the death of Jesus rather than on the Romans who actually performed the crucifixion.

The brief introduction of Peter (verse 54) will be followed up in the next section. Is his agitated lack of affirmation before the accusers to be contrasted with Jesus' silence and straight statements?

The witnesses cannot agree in their evidence. The whole trial is portrayed as a perversion of justice and even the charge of blasphemy (verse 64) is wrong since claims to Messiahship did not constitute grounds for blasphemy. Jesus does acknowledge who he is, in terms probably used by the Marcan Church: Christ, the Son of the Blessed (God). The question put to him is answered in terms of Daniel 7.13, Psalm 110.1 and the Son of man; and Mark's congregation would have been struck by the reference to his 'coming with the clouds of heaven' (verse 62).

The high priest cannot contain himself and performs, somewhat inappropriately, the judicial act of tearing his clothes. For him, and for them all, Jesus is guilty and deserving of death. He is despised and rejected, abused, maltreated and ridiculed. He is deliberately and unjustly condemned.

In summary, if this is a just trial, Jesus is clearly innocent. But this is not a just trial. Jesus stands before self-confessed enemies, ironically the men of God who cannot recognise what is happening. Jesus makes his confession but attempts no other justification or self-defence. Otherwise he is silent before his accusers. He is subjected to ridicule, rejection and suffering, just as he predicted.

Peter's Denial   Mark 14.66 – 72

Earlier in Mark's Gospel, Peter had been the first to make the great confession, 'You are the Christ'(8.29). After that great moment at Caesarea Philippi, Jesus then went on to tell them what this would mean for him in terms of suffering, death and resurrection. Peter protests at such ideas but has to be rebuked by Jesus for uttering satanic thoughts. Jesus' suffering is inevitable and, more than that, those who follow him will suffer also – and what of the person who is ashamed of this Christ?

Now the story of Peter's denial is bluntly told and many scholars suggest it came from the reminiscences of Peter himself. Given his standing in the early Church no one would have made up the report of such a failure! The maid asks a simple enough question. It does not need a long confession by way of answer, only honesty. But Peter fails the time of testing. He is ashamed, first of Jesus, but at the end of himself. His tears are bitter.

Perhaps Mark tells the story above all because the words of Jesus are fulfilled. The hope which this brings is more important than any moralising about the need to take every opportunity to witness, however true that might be.

Jesus before Pilate   Mark 15.1 – 15

For Jesus to have been brought before the Roman

governor the charges against him must have had some political content, perhaps stating that he was a threat to public order, that his popularity had revolutionary overtones.

Mark says that Jesus was 'handed over' (verse 1, *Good News Bible*) to Pilate. Later (verse 15) Pilate hands Jesus over to be crucified. This phrase became almost technical in character as the early Christians spoke of the death of Jesus. Behind its use is the sense that those who do the hand-over are, unwittingly but nonetheless, God's agents.

Pilate asks if Jesus is the King of the Jews and Jesus' answer reads strangely. We must realise that whatever answer he gave would be troublesome, because the same word can be heard in different ways by different ears. Jesus remains silent before his accusers, a point we have noted before, but we ought also to note that Pilate 'wondered', a word that has a religious tone. Jesus' silence speaks of his will to suffer. It is an **awesome** silence that bears its own witness.

Very little, if anything, is known about the custom of releasing a prisoner at the feast although, presumably, the governor could always grant a pardon if he wished. What is clear for Mark is that Pilate can find no fault in Jesus. He is innocent of the charges brought against him. There is nothing in law to prevent Pilate releasing Jesus.

Nothing in law – but the pressure is on. Pilate has seen through the action of the Jewish leaders (verse 10) but the crowd is being whipped up by the chief priests. Mark is quite clear where the responsibility lies. The crowd calls for Barabbas' release and the killing of Jesus. Some scholars see 'the crowd' as standing, in Mark's mind, for the whole Jewish nation.

Once again (verse 14) the Roman authority asserts

Jesus' innocence but this only incites the crowd further. Pilate is being heavily leaned on. Mark does not tell us of the hand-washing (Matthew 27.24), only of Pilate's legal judgement of Jesus' innocence and then of his delivering Jesus to be crucified.

Once more the Roman authorities are portrayed as having no direct quarrel with Jesus. They see him neither as trouble nor a threat to trouble. The responsibility for the death of Jesus is thrust on the Jews whose hatred of Jesus is unwarranted. In the face of all this Jesus keeps silent and he goes further on the journey to death **because he is the Messiah**.

The soldiers make mock   Mark 15.16 – 20

Some scholars suggest that this section is a Marcan insertion. It is not found in Luke. However, it reads naturally and carries forward some of the important themes we have already noticed.

In these verses are echoes of Isaiah 53. Perhaps now is the time to read that chapter about the one despised and rejected, the one who bore the sins of many, who was wounded, who was silent. The fulfilment theme we noticed earlier is still being worked out.

The soldiers mock Jesus. He wears one of their cloaks and the crown of thorns is pushed on his head not so much as a torture as for mocking this 'royalty'. They make game of him. His dignity is ridiculed.

We observe again the emphasis on 'the King of the Jews'. He suffers all of this because he is the Messiah, not in spite of it. We notice how passive Jesus is – everything is done to him, he receives the mocking and the punishment – and all the time he is silent, 'like a sheep . . . before its shearers' (Isaiah 53.7). For Jesus to resist would be to resist the awful will of God.

The crucifixion   Mark 15.21 – 32

The soldiers now lead Jesus out to put him to death. The Roman way is crucifixion, cruel, long and brutal. Mark says that Simon of Cyrene, in North Africa, is compelled to carry Jesus' cross. Is Jesus exhausted from the beating? Simon is introduced without explanation and reference is made to his two sons, Alexander and Rufus. Are they now well-known as church members? Is this the Rufus of Romans 16.13? The detail is another way by which Mark shows his congregation the trust-worthiness of his information.

The Greek word used in verse 21 for 'carry' is the same word used in Mark 8.34, a saying which describes discipleship as 'taking up the cross and following'.

They come to Golgotha. It was the custom for the prosperous women of Jerusalem to offer condemned criminals a drugged drink to dull the pain (see Proverbs 31.6 – 7). Jesus refuses this help. He faces out his suffer-ings, in all their fullness, to the end.

They crucified him' – that is all Mark says about the deed. There is no attempt to talk up the horror. The report is blunt and direct.

The reference to the soldiers dividing Jesus' garments is a clear illustration of the early Christians' emphasis that what happened to Jesus is the fulfilment of Scripture – read Psalm 22. Read Psalm 69 as well.

Those condemned to crucifixion usually had some placard making public the reason for their execution. For the fifth and final time in **Mark** the phrase 'King of the Jews' is used. In Mark's Gospel, Jesus dies as the Messiah, surrounded by robbers (Isaiah 53.12).

The onlookers now begin their taunts. The charges against Jesus of threatening the temple and claiming to be the Messiah are brought up again. They call for Jesus to come down from the cross, to save his own life, to work a miracle. But Jesus has already said that whoever seeks to save his life will lose it (8.35). It is because he is the Christ that he cannot come down. He must stay, suffer and die. This is the way of God's salvation. Mark's readers had to reflect on and live with this unthinkable fact.

Jesus breathes his last   Mark 15.33 – 39

Jesus was crucified at the third hour (verse 25). Now, at the sixth hour (noon), there comes darkness covering the whole land for three more hours. The darkness is a symbol, heavy with judgement. Something cosmic is happening.

Then Jesus utters the great cry of God-forsakenness. It is the only word from the cross which Mark records. Its meaning is ambiguous, perhaps deliberately so. Its most natural reading for us is of utter despair. Jesus enters into the depths of aloneness, abandonment. The total horror of his cross overwhelms him. It is as if God has forsaken him.

But we ought also to note that his cry is the opening line of Psalm 22. We have already noticed the significance of this psalm for Mark's account of the passion. Although it begins in this despairing way it is, in fact, the prayer of a just and trusting servant who looks in faith for the loving protection of God and his vindication. Both of these interpretations are worth much reflection.

Some in the crowd mishear '*Eloi*' for Elijah, the forerunner of the Messiah and one who, it is believed, comes when God's people need assistance. They wonder whether even now there will be a miracle for

Jesus and he will be taken down from the cross. But they wonder in vain.

Jesus utters a loud cry and breathes his last. Again the language is direct with no romantic embellishments. Mark leaves us with the impression that Jesus gives up his life. It is not snatched from him. He breathes it out as an offering.

And the curtain of the temple is split apart. Again the significance is not clear – or perhaps we should say it is rich with interpretation. It could mean that a barrier is removed, between God and all of us. Or it could mean that the division between Jew and Gentile is destroyed by the death of Jesus.

So we are brought to a great climax in the Gospel. The centurion, Rome's representative, responsible for over-seeing this death, sees what others have failed to see, and says, 'Truly this man was the Son of God!' He grasps what others had failed to see at Jesus' baptism and transfiguration (1.11; 9.7). It is significant that a Gentile, a Roman, proclaims this truth. He sees that this Jesus, despised and forsaken, is the Son of God or Messiah. He sees this truth at the cross.

For the Jews, anyone who was hanged on a tree was cursed. How could anyone who suffers and dies in this way be in the purposes of God? A cross spoke of judgement and disaster, or so the tradition had it. But so much about God and his ways had to be rethought in the light of Jesus and the cross. He is Messiah **because** he suffered and died. The foolishness of God is wiser than human wisdom (from 1 Corinthians 1.25).

The women, the burial and the tomb   Mark 15.40 – 47

Thus far Mark has given no particular place to women in his Gospel, and now, rather suddenly, they are brought to the fore. This is probably another indication of Mark's emphasis on firsthand testimony. The women are said to have looked on from afar, again emphasising the isolation of Jesus from all human help and sympathy. They watch him die.

It seems to be important to Mark to make it quite clear that Jesus was truly dead and buried. The resurrection would prompt all kinds of rumours, so what appears here as insignificant details are important. Joseph of Arimathea is unknown apart from this incident. He is a member of the Jewish Council (Sanhedrin) and Mark describes him as one who 'was looking for the kingdom of God'. This may mean he shared the hope that was kindled by Jesus and that he was in some sense a disciple. Or perhaps he was simply a pious Jew who looked to do right and tried in all aspects of life to fulfil the law (Deuteronomy 21.22 – 23). Whatever the status of Joseph was, he provides the burial-place and sees that the body of Jesus is laid to rest.

Verses 44 – 45 are omitted by Matthew and Luke. They underline Mark's sharp insistence on Jesus being well and truly dead. So, with Pilate's permission, the body is taken down by human hands and hastily wrapped in the shroud with no time for anointing. The tomb is sealed with the rock and the two Marys see where Jesus is laid. There can be no suggestion that they went to the wrong tomb on the Sunday morning.

Some special emphases

In chapter one the ways in which three different congregations kept Good Friday were described. Each told the same story but with different emphases according to their insights and situation. Given the way Mark tells the story of the crucifixion, what special emphases were there in Mark's congregation? We can discern at least seven important points.

✝ There is an undoubted stress on Jesus' suffering. There were some congregations in the early Church who concentrated so much on the triumph of the resurrection that the cross tended to lose its great significance. Mark insists on the importance of the crucifixion. In his Gospel he spends much more time telling the story of the cross than that of the empty tomb. You could say that the whole theme of his Gospel is summed up in the cross. There is a necessity in it all. Jesus **must** suffer.

✝ This '**must**' is related to what Mark believes is God's will. We have noticed the importance of the Old Testament Scriptures, especially Psalms 22, 38, 69 and Isaiah 53. The Scriptures declare God's will, God's surprising will in this case, that the Messiah must suffer.

✝ So, at one level, Jesus dies because it is the way God's purposes are worked out. At another level, Mark seems determined to show that Jesus died because of Jewish opposition and pressure. We have noted how the Romans, in the person of Pilate, recognise Jesus' innocence. He has done nothing deserving of death. Jesus is crucified because of overwhelming Jewish pressure. If Mark's congregation is in Rome, or anywhere in a Gentile environment where there is opposition and threat, it would be important to hear that their leader was not condemned by the Roman authorities. They could find no fault in him. They would have let him go. They realised that it was only out of envy that he was before them anyway.

✝ Mark leaves his readers in no doubt that Jesus died. There are references that seem to say to his readers, 'These things are true, some of the family of the people mentioned are present with you. They can verify these eyewitness accounts.' Certainly later in the Church's history some tried to say that Jesus was not truly a man and that he did not actually die. Mark would deny both points. He asserts that Jesus was as much a human being as any of us and he really did die on the cross.

✝ A recurring point in Mark's Gospel is the disciples' total lack of understanding. They fail to grasp the point of the parables. They seem bemused by Jesus' teaching. They do not stand by him when suffering comes, as if what is happening is a surprise and utterly incomprehensible to them. But part of what Mark's account of the crucifixion of Jesus involves is some solid teaching on discipleship. Discipleship means suffering, a point that would not have been lost by those Christians who were Nero's victims. Every time Mark records Jesus' passion predictions (8.31; 9.31; 10.32 – 34) he says that the disciples do not understand. Also, on each occasion, there follows some teaching on the conditions of true discipleship as being service, taking up the cross, giving or losing your life as the way to true life. Discipleship is a costly business but no one should be surprised at that. If the Master had to suffer so much, why should the disciple be surprised if his or her way were costly too?

✝ However, it was a surprise because it was still difficult for many to understand how Jesus could be both the Messiah and the one who hangs on the tree. For those with a Jewish background it was tantamount to contradiction to speak of a crucified Messiah

(1 Corinthians 1.23). They believed that those who were crucified were accursed. And, for the Greeks, the very suggestion that God's eternal purposes might be worked out in this way was just utter foolishness. Mark's point all along is that Jesus is the King of the Jews, the Son of God, not in spite of his suffering and cruel death but because of it. The Old Testament, when it is properly read, gives indications of all this or so Mark's church would argue.

In the early part of Mark's Gospel, up to 8.26, there are many stories of Jesus performing miracles, exorcisms, healings and other mighty works. The casual reader might be tempted to think that Jesus is a great wonder-worker, a good preacher with a popular line in miracles. But this would be sadly to misunderstand him and God's way of revealing his saving purpose for the world. The chief priests and the crowd show their blindness when they call on Jesus to do something spectacular, 'Come down now from the cross, that we may see and believe' (15.32).

Mark rejects a 'sign and wonder' Christology. For him the meaning of what God is about is only fully revealed when Jesus dies, abused, rejected and alone. He uses a Roman centurion to declare that this crucified man is the Son of God.

✝ Although it does not come out so strongly in the passion narrative, one other theme is certainly there in Mark's Gospel. It is that of vindication, of the Son of man coming in great glory (14.62). The hard teaching on costly discipleship was not without strong affirmations of hope and victory (9.1). This too would have mattered to Mark's congregation as they were put to the sword. How long, Lord? The promise of his coming was part of the Good News, even if he who comes, and he who triumphs, must first carry the cross. You have to give life before you can receive it back. That God will come to vindicate his own is an important theme for Mark and his church.

Some personal reflections

The last few paragraphs of this chapter are personal reflections on Mark's story of the crucifixion. I have tried to 'listen' to the text again and this is something of what I have 'heard' from Mark today.

First, I am drawn again into the mystery of Christ's death. Mark has laid heavy emphasis on the divine necessity of the cross, 'the Son of man must suffer'. I wonder about that. Was there no other way for God to take? I cannot answer that question but, as a Christian believer, I hold that this cross is no accident. It is God's cross in our world. Suffering love, giving oneself for others and for God, appears as God's way of salvation. This is what the cross reveals. There is a great mystery here that, above all, evokes worship. The cross is the key to our Christian understanding not simply of ourselves but of God. A theology that bypasses Golgotha will be on the wrong road. It will have missed the way.

This happens too easily. Our thought of God is often shaped in terms of power, majesty, strength and victory. Mark was aware in his day of how people could seek a Christ 'after their own image'. So they looked for the miracle merchant, or the forceful leader, even the military champion. False Christs had already come to trouble the Church. They illustrate my point of warning that we all are tempted to see and seek the Christ we desire. Some people shaped a Christology that avoided the cross both for Jesus and themselves. That may still

be the temptation as power ministries, wrong understandings of signs and wonders, instant spiritual
growth and much else reflect the secular spirit of the
age with its forceful dominant notions of leadership,
growth and success. Against these the suffering servant Messiah seems so frail, literally pushed over in the
power squeeze between the priests and Pilate. We are
given a Christ who suffers for us and with us. To long
for more is to ask for less.

Then, inevitably, I am led to reflect on the cost of
discipleship. There are those who know this better than
I. Even today Christians are falsely accused in unjust
courts. They are wrongly condemned, imprisoned and
some join the noble army of martyrs. Let us pray for
those who suffer now for the divine purpose. They bear
a witness to the world and to the Church.

I come back to Mark's picture of Jesus. Increasingly
Jesus is alone. His friends desert, betray, deny him. He
stands before his accusers, knowing their fearsome
power, and he is silent. He attempts no self-
justification, no compromising explanation. Around
him are people who are themselves being pressurised.
They are the fraught ones. They scheme and struggle.
He stands silent and trusts himself to God. Even at the
worst moment of all, when the forsakenness is utterly
overwhelming, his cry is to God. He waits for what
God will surely bring and in that trust he gives up his
life. It all happened on a Friday, but Sunday was even
then on its way. Is this what faith always means? Is this
what we are called to? A radical trust in the purposes of
God, obediently walking the way appointed, seeking
no self-justification or special concession, only bearing
the cross until the day breaks and God's strong mercy
is revealed? Jesus appears in weakness, rejection and
great suffering. But compared with Pilate and the

priests he is already the free man. He knows that the service of God is perfect freedom.

A prayer

Living God, in strong trust and quiet obedience your Son Jesus Christ set his face towards Jerusalem, receiving the insults, taking the pain, bearing the cross. We pray for all who suffer in your cause today. We pray for ourselves that we may be faithful as we take up the cross and wait for that day when all your purposes will be complete in Christ. Amen.

Some questions and suggestions for further thought

1 What has struck you in your reading of Mark's account of the crucifixion? Why are these features important for you?

2 Why do we think that Judas' betrayal is more serious than Peter's denial? In what ways do we deny Christ?

3 Why did antagonism build up against Jesus? Think of situations in today's world where hatred and fear are fuelled. Why does this happen?

4 Simon was compelled to carry the cross. Can anyone be compelled to carry the cross? Mark says that Jesus must suffer. What is the difference between the compulsion laid on Simon and that of Jesus?

5 Why do you think that Jesus '**must**' suffer?

6 Try to find out about someone who is suffering for their faith in God today. Pray for them. Is there anything else you can do – for example, write them a letter?

3
Matthew's story of the cross

Jesus was a Jew, as were his twelve disciples. His death, resurrection, and the giving of the Holy Spirit, were all events in Jerusalem, the holy city. Yet it is very easy for us to overlook the Jewishness of Jesus and this fundamental context for the early Church.

It seems that in the earliest days of the Church there was no great break with the synagogue or the temple. The first disciples kept up their attendance at the temple (Acts 2.46) and in many ways lived as a group within Judaism but with the all-important conviction that the Messiah had come. Very quickly, however, differences emerged both in the Gentile world where Paul was so effective as a missionary and also in Palestine. Palestinian Christianity, understandably enough, retained its Jewishness longer than the Gentile congregations. None of us can utterly escape from the influence of our background, nor would we wish to if we had been born and raised as Jews, knowing the Scriptures, and now thankful the Messiah had come.

In AD 66 – 70 there occurred in Palestine what is often called the Jewish War. It was the last revolt against the Roman occupation but the result was disaster for the Jews. They were defeated, humiliated and, most significantly, the temple was destroyed. The unthinkable had happened. It was an important event for Jews and Christians alike.

Many Jews fled from Jerusalem. The leadership in the nation's religious life passed to the Pharisees, an essentially lay movement, whose base was the synagogues, whose love was for the law of God and whose desire was for righteousness. Many of these Pharisees were noble, godly, sincere and worthy Jews. It seems that an important centre of 'rabbinical Judaism' was established after the war in Jamnia, a town in north-west Judah. There the community worked hard at reading the Scriptures and reforming Jewish life based on the Sabbath and synagogue.

What has this to do with Matthew? First, we must concede that if we knew little for certain about Mark and his community we know even less about Matthew.

From a reading of the Gospel we can at least discern that the book makes full use of Mark. It is a church book, the only one of the four Gospels to use the word 'church'. It is clearly concerned with the relationship between the story of Jesus and the Old Testament from which Matthew often quotes, usually to show how what has happened is a fulfilment of earlier statements. There is an awareness that the Church has a mission to go into all the world but especially to the house of Israel. Also there is a powerful teaching element in the book, as if Matthew were providing procedures for church affairs, with clear teaching on discipleship, righteousness and the meaning of what God has done in Jesus.

Therefore, perhaps Matthew represents a church aware of its roots, concerned with its mission, careful of its way of life and conscious of its growing distinction from Judaism. Matthew's Christianity has strong links with Palestinian rather than Gentile forms. Perhaps the Gospel he writes is in conscious separation from Jamnia. The debates, which Jesus is pictured as having with the Jewish leaders of his day, may well tell us also about the dialogue, or lack of it, between Church and synagogue as Matthew experienced it.

Matthew is, possibly, a Jew by upbringing. Perhaps he has been baptised and become a Christian in company with others, both Jew and Gentile. As they steadily become a distinct group, so the full suspicion and resentment from their neighbours, Jew and Gentile, is turned upon them. Maybe the congregation gathers in a large city in a region where the Christian movement has rapidly grown numerically, perhaps in northern Palestine or Syria.

Matthew writes as a teacher, perhaps especially for other Christian teachers. His church takes discipleship seriously as befits the greater righteousness (5.20), and the ethical demands, fellowship obligations and disciplines are all taken seriously. What does distinctively Christian existence involve? What is new about the new covenant? What should be the Christian attitude to the Torah, the Sabbath and the synagogue? And now that Christianity is separating from Judaism what is its role in the world and how should its policy be formulated?

With these things in mind let us turn to Matthew's way of describing the crucifixion of Jesus.

Jesus is arrested   Matthew 26.47 – 56

Matthew basically follows Mark's account with some slight differences. Judas makes a more definite approach to Jesus. He seems to have a slightly higher profile. Jesus asks, 'Friend, why are you here?' and to all who know the story the word 'friend' has a rather ironic sound. What is the status of this one of the twelve?

The one who draws the sword and is violent is described as 'one of those who were with' Jesus – in other words, a disciple. So perhaps we should read

Jesus' reply as being to all disciples, the Church, those who are 'with him'. To resort to force is the way of self-destruction. Jesus rebukes the one who would fight the enemy. If need be he could call not on twelve disciples but on twelve legions of angels, the battalions of heaven, to come to his defence. But that would be wrong because it would frustrate God's will (26.54). Jesus rejects any kind of intervention on his behalf. He will be obedient to the divine purpose. This is more important than his own life.

Matthew also records Jesus as saying that the crowd had come out against him as if he were a dangerous criminal. Why did they not take him when he was teaching? What else has he done but teach? Once again Matthew stresses the fulfilment element in what is taking place.

There is no reference to the naked young man, only the reference to the disciples quickly disappearing from the scene.

Already we are brought face to face with some of Matthew's emphases. The rejection and death of Jesus will happen because this is the will of God. It could be temporarily frustrated by those who do not perceive the Father's will but, because Jesus knows the Father, he will trust himself fully to that purpose. He will be obedient. Matthew is not just reporting the facts of Jesus' betrayal and crucifixion. He is showing, with reference to the Scriptures, how God's purposeful design is being worked out. At this stage only the one who knows the Father (11.27) is aware of the real meaning of these necessary events.

Before the Sanhedrin   Matthew 26.57 – 68

Matthew, unlike Mark, identifies the high priest as

Caiaphas. Bluntly it is said that the Council sought 'false testimony' but Matthew will emphasise that Jesus is judged and condemned on the grounds of his claiming to be the Messiah. So two witnesses come forward 'at last' (26.60), two being necessary for validity (Deuteronomy 17.6).

The reference to the temple of God is more direct in Matthew (remember the destruction of the temple in AD 70). The high priest puts Jesus on oath, 'I adjure you by the living God, tell us if you are the Christ, the Son of God' (verse 63). Jesus replies, 'You have said so', and in that reply confirms the content of the question. He is the Christ and 'hereafter . . . the Son of man' will be seen 'seated at the right hand of Power, and coming on the clouds of heaven' (26.64). Matthew is indicating the relationship between Jesus' death and glory.

For the high priest this claim to be the Messiah is blasphemy and the penalty is death. This would certainly be a bone of contention between Matthew's church and the Pharisees of his day.

Matthew records Jesus being slapped and abused, adding the title 'Christ' from the lips of the accusers. The whole passage has an ironic sense for they call him what he is.

Matthew emphasises Christ's authority; and shows that Jesus, by his actions, has given an inspiring example to his disciples. Matthew also suggests, more directly than Mark, that the way to the cross is the path to glory.

Peter's denial   Matthew 26.69 – 75; 27.1 – 2

Peter has an undeniably special place in Matthew's

Gospel. He is set first among the disciples (10.2). The story of his denial is told by Matthew in a terse form.

The charge against Peter is that he has been 'with Jesus', a phrase we have already noticed is tantamount to saying 'disciple'. After his first denial in the court-yard, Peter moves out to the porch, perhaps symbolically away from being with Jesus. We should also note that his denial is 'before them all' (see 10.33) and that his denial is 'with an oath' (see 5.34).

Peter, hearing the cock crow, goes out and weeps bitterly. It is only after Jesus' confession before the authorities that Matthew tells the story of Peter's denial. Matthew's church will be inspired by the example of Jesus, but Peter will stand as a warning for all who are challenged to confess their faith.

Matthew briefly concludes the 'trial' before the Sanhedrin and informs his readers that Jesus is delivered, bound, to Pilate the governor (27.1–2). There is an element of fulfilment here because in his passion prediction Jesus has said that the Son of man will be delivered to the Gentiles (20.18–19).

The death of Judas   Matthew 27.3–10

This is a strange section, found only in Matthew and telling a different story from that of Acts 1.16–20. What is the point of this passage?

On the surface it reads as an effort to 'tidy up', to fill a gap left in Mark's account. What did happen to Judas? There would be a natural, if morbid, curiosity in the question. But Matthew is not writing to meet his readers' curiosity. Knowing what happened to Judas is hardly going to deepen the readers' awareness of God's salvation in Christ.

There is a form of Jewish writing called Midrash. It usually begins from a passage of Scripture and attempts to interpret its meaning. Often what is written is handled in creative ways, to deduce new insights into religious life. So, before looking again at this passage from Matthew, we might usefully read Zechariah 11.4 – 17; 2 Samuel 17.23 (the only other suicide mentioned in the Bible) and Jeremiah 19 and 32.

That is a lot of background reading but it helps to explain the passage in Matthew. The Gospel writer is not trying to provide information about the death of Judas. Rather this is just another illustration of his general approach – that is, showing how all that happened to Jesus is part of God's will. Jesus' own prophetic word about the one who would betray him is fulfilled (Matthew 26.24).

We should also notice Matthew's implication that, in receiving back the 'blood money', the Jewish leaders are accepting responsibility for Jesus' death. Further, these verses underline what will be a growing theme, that of Jesus' innocence.

There is also something for us to reflect on in the contrast between two failed disciples. Both Peter and Judas show remorse. Judas tries to make amends even to the extent of taking his own life. But nothing can turn aside denial and betrayal – and put an end to tears – except the divine mercy which is beyond price.

Jesus before Pilate   Matthew 27.11 – 26

The prisoner stands before his judge. The question is, 'Are you the King of the Jews?' This is the central question. But Jesus virtually remains silent and Matthew, like Mark, stresses Pilate's argument with him.

The incident of Barabbas is retold in a style similar to

that in Mark. However, a number of changes emphasise the direct choice between Jesus and the notorious prisoner, and the consequent, conscious rejection of Jesus 'who is called Christ'. The language underlines that Jesus is not dealt with as a political figure. It is as Messiah that he is rejected. Pilate is aware of the injustice and envy at work in the crowd led by the chief priests and the elders.

The reference to Pilate's wife is made by Matthew alone. She is troubled in a dream because of 'that righteous man'. Does the reference to the dream suggest that her seeing Jesus has divine origin? It would not be the first time, in Matthew's Gospel, that pagan Gentiles are led to the truth – remember the Magi (2.1 – 12).

Pilate makes the choice explicit, Jesus or Barabbas, and the crowd all call for the crucifixion of the one 'who is called Christ'. What more can Pilate do? There is a riot beginning, neither Pilate or Jesus has provoked it, but political expediency will, perhaps, cool it. So Pilate washes his hands, a gesture later affirmed in words declaring his innocence of whatever happens to Jesus (Deuteronomy 21.1 – 9).

Matthew seems to be concerned with showing, beyond all doubt, where the responsibility for the death of Jesus lies. In verse 25 that responsibility is taken by the Jewish people, who reject the Messiah. So Pilate releases Barabbas. Matthew omits Mark's phrase about Pilate doing so to satisfy the crowd. For Matthew, Barabbas' release and Jesus' crucifixion are the result of the people's deliberate and clear choice.

The soldiers mock Jesus   Matthew 27.27 – 31

Matthew's account is more descriptive and vivid than

Mark's. Jesus is mocked for claiming royal status: 'Hail, King of the Jews!' The scarlet cloak, the crown, the reed in the right hand, the kneeling and the address all parody a coronation. The way Matthew recounts these actions carries with it a heavier atmosphere of increasing violence. Jesus is abused, ironically for what he really is.

The crucifixion   Matthew 27.32 – 44

Before we consider Matthew's story of the crucifixion, it is worth looking back to his account of the parable of the vineyard. Notice that he has rearranged Mark's version of this (compare Matthew 21.39 with Mark 12.8) by stating that the son was cast out of the vineyard and then killed. Matthew has done this so that the parable agrees with the account of the crucifixion and follows his fulfilment theme.

Simon of Cyrene is mentioned, but not his sons, presumably because they were not known to Matthew's church. As in Mark, Simon is compelled to carry the cross. Look up Matthew 5.41, can any one be 'compelled' to carry the cross as a disciple?

Jesus is offered wine mingled with gall – a slight change from Mark's account but following Psalm 69.21 and so emphasising Matthew's theme of fulfilment. The same theme is there in the soldiers casting lots for the garments of the victim (Psalm 22.18). Once more we notice how the Gospel writer simply and starkly reports Jesus' crucifixion.

The way Matthew describes the inscription 'This is Jesus the King of the Jews' (verse 37) makes it sound more definite, formal, authoritative and final.

He highlights the theme of mockery. The passers-by, the chief priests and elders, the robbers, all pour out their scorn. The charge about destroying the temple is revived (verse 40). Matthew's readers will know that the old Jewish order based on the temple has come to an end already.

We ought to pay careful attention to the charge, 'If you are the Son of God' (verse 40). For Matthew, there is a special relationship between Jesus and the Father. He is the Son. But this phrase, 'If you are . . .' has been used before, in the temptations (4.1 – 11) and in the trial before the Sanhedrin (26.63). It is a demonic temptation, to exploit his standing in a way that is not in God's purposes. The chief priests show their blindness by saying that if Jesus will come down from the cross they will believe in him (verse 42).

Verse 43 occurs only in Matthew and echoes Psalm 22.8 and the Wisdom of Solomon 2.12 – 20. This is the theme of the mocking of a righteous man, who is dismissed by all, given over to suffering but who still trusts in God. This is Matthew's theme. The mockery only adds to the high tension, all the higher because of Matthew's emphasis on who Jesus is.

Jesus yields up his spirit   Matthew 27.45 – 50

'There was darkness over all the land.' Matthew uses different Greek wording from Mark. Some scholars suggest that behind Matthew's change there is Exodus 10.22, the plague of darkness over all the land, the last plague before the death of the first-born. There may also be an echo of Amos 8.9.

Another change Matthew makes is in verse 49. Mark has some people suggesting that everyone waits to see if Elijah will come and take Jesus down from the cross, where Matthew has 'save him'. The following verses, with their references to events of cosmic proportions, bear testimony that this is God coming to save Jesus.

Jesus 'yielded up his spirit'. Again a change from Mark's 'breathed his last'. Matthew conveys a greater sense of Jesus willingly giving his all to God. The voluntary nature of Jesus' action is what is underlined. He has surrendered himself totally to God. He has obeyed the Father in quiet trust.

Immediate effects   Matthew 27.51 – 54

Mark mentioned two 'signs' following the death of Jesus, the rending of the temple curtain and the con- fession of the centurion. Matthew has rather more to say.

He speaks of events that for the Jews would have been immediately linked in their minds with the inbreaking of the great Messianic age – earthquakes, splitting rocks, opening tombs, resurrection of the dead and the return of saints to Jerusalem (Ezekiel 37.12 – 14).

All this is, to say the least, spectacular and it is sur- prising that the other Gospel writers missed what only Matthew records. An argument, about whether it really happened, will be inconclusive since our decision will depend on our prior presuppositions as to how we should read the Bible. What is really important is that Matthew used these signs to signify the meaning of Jesus' death.

The rending of the temple curtain signifies the end of the old order and the beginning of a new and living way.

The raising of the saints signifies that the suffering of the just and obedient people of Israel, who have died, is here vindicated and fulfilled in the death of Jesus (although the phrase 'after his resurrection' gives Jesus' resurrection the proper priority).

The confession and the reaction of the centurion, and those who were with him, signify an event of divine power. When they say, 'Truly this was the Son of God', they are not announcing anything new but only confirming what was the truth. Matthew declares the faith of the Christian community and the fulfilment of the Scriptures (8.10 – 12).

The women, the burial and the tomb
Matthew 27.55 – 61

Matthew portrays the women as real disciples, and he identifies Joseph as being both rich and a disciple. The interest Matthew has in the burial of Jesus is underlined by reference to the 'new' tomb and the careful reference to the witnesses. The women 'were sitting opposite the sepulchre'. There can be no possibility of their mistakenly going to the wrong tomb later.

The guards are posted   Matthew 27.62 – 66

In Matthew's time, and since, people have suggested that the whole Christian gospel of the resurrection rests on a deception. Perhaps the women went to the wrong tomb: we have seen how Matthew responded to that. Perhaps the disciples came and stole the body: Matthew tells of the guard set by Pilate at the request of the Jews. The claim that the tomb was empty is not disputed, only the explanation of its emptiness. Matthew is countering the charges brought against the message his church proclaims. The answer only heightens the claim that this is the activity of God.

Some special emphases

It has become commonplace in twentieth-century Britain for Christians to say we are in a missionary situation and so must work out our faith and discipleship in a context of competing faiths and ideologies. In fact, of course, Christians have always been in that kind of situation. Certainly Matthew's church had to walk the path of discipleship in close company with Judaism and the various religions of the Gentiles. Theirs was a challenging situation for, like any minority group, they would have had tense moments.

We have already remarked on the Jewishness of Matthew's Gospel and this fact must be fully recognised when we come to look at the special emphases of Matthew and his church. These emphases are inter-related but, for convenience of identification and understanding, they are dealt with separately.

✝ In Matthew's Gospel the theme of fulfilment is important. Again and again reference is made to the Old Testament, directly or indirectly. Matthew 26.56 is typical, 'All this has taken place, that the scriptures of the prophets might be fulfilled.' What is primarily at issue here, as in Mark's Gospel, is a conviction that what Jesus did, and what was done to him, is God working out his purpose.

For someone with a Jewish background, and that may well include Matthew and a good number of his readers, the story of the cross is a great stumbling-block. It must have appeared as a colossal accident, a horrible freak fracture that threatens to frustrate the divine plan which only the great energy of resurrection can put right and bring God out on top again. But Matthew does not see it like that. All of Jesus' life, death as well as resurrection is what God willed. If only

53

the ancient people had really listened to the prophets and heard what they had said they would have been prepared for this strange work.

✝ If only they had listened. However, Matthew is quite clear that the Jewish people, the chief priests, scribes, elders and the crowds have not perceived the truth. They have not simply rejected the Messiah. They are responsible for his death – 'his blood be on us and on our children'(27.25). There is tragedy here because Jesus was sent to the lost sheep of the house of Israel, and his disciples were to 'go nowhere among the Gentiles'(10.5). An anti-Jewish theme is present in Matthew. Perhaps his church knows, years later on, what it is to be harrassed by those who blame the minority Christian group for tragedies that have befallen the nation. Matthew is direct in his approach. The Jews have full responsibility for the death of the Messiah. Such an accusation must have hurt both the accused and Matthew, the Jewish Christian accuser.

✝ Like Mark, Matthew proclaims Jesus as the Son of God. But this comes through in a more definite way in Matthew's Gospel. It is because Jesus is the Son of God that his ministry leads to his death. The devil comes to him at the temptations (4.3,6) with the same taunt that is there at the cross, 'If you are the Son of God . . .' Matthew affirms this relationship, thus giving a meaning to divine sonship that goes deeper than Mark's. Moreover, because Jesus is the Son he becomes the one by whom we also can call God, Father.

✝ The Christ of Matthew's Gospel knows God's forsakenness and painful mockery. Matthew makes no direct references to the suffering servant songs of Isaiah but crucial to his thinking is the Son of God who experiences forsakenness. Perhaps Matthew's church knew what it was to be mocked and abused for their faith.

✝ For all that, there is something majestic about the figure of Christ in Matthew's passion story. He has authority and power, greater than that of the plotting priests and pliable Pilate. He could call down the legions of angels but he stands alone, silent, the one who knows what is happening. There is powerful force in Matthew's insistence, 'This is the King of the Jews.'

✝ Let us recall those strange verses, following the death of Jesus, when the earthquake splits the rocks, the temple curtain is torn, the dead are raised and the centurion recognises the Son of God. These are events that speak of the presence of God. An event of cosmic proportions is taking place and for Matthew it marks the beginning of world mission. No longer will the children of God be found only among the house of Israel. The entire Jewish leadership is present to witness their tragedy, which is also God's redeeming work for Jews and Gentiles. It is no surprise to find Matthew's story of Jesus ending with the command to go into all the world (28.16 – 20).

✝ Disciples are identified in this Gospel as those who have been with Jesus. But the Gospel has also spoken of Emmanuel (1.23), of Christ being with those who meet in his name (18.20) and even of his presence with disciples to the end of the age (28.20). The message of the crucifixion of the Son of God is both a word of hope and abiding encouragement to persist in discipleship regardless of what the world might seek to do.

Some personal reflections

Reflecting on Matthew's account of the crucifixion raises for me two paradoxes, two of those conundrums that seem to be an integral part of the story of Jesus.

The first is in the contrast of majesty and apparent powerlessness. Jesus is seen in more regal terms by Matthew than by Mark. It is also part of Matthew's understanding of Jesus that he could virtually do anything, such were the resources of power open to him. But the twelve legions of angels, the power to produce stupendous signs, these are not used by Jesus. The paradox is that this weakness is strength, this unwillingness to engage in power-play, on the world's terms, turns out to be the overcoming of just that type of power. Jesus is a more authoritative person than Pilate or the chief priests, yet he is their victim and their victor.

For Matthew's church, and the church of every generation, this raises questions about the Christian's involvement in the struggles of the world. Jesus was crucified by a combination of political and religious powers. He stood against them passively to the end. So why did they hound him to death? Clearly because he was some kind of challenge to their position, beliefs and values. His teachings had implicit criticisms of their injustice and unrighteousness. Jesus being the person he was, it was inevitable that there would be trouble. He was powerful, but paradoxically his power was in his weakness, in his very refusal not to play their game.

The second paradox echoes an emphasis of Mark. It is between responsibility and purpose. In his many references Matthew stresses that what was taking place was in God's will and purpose, to which Jesus gave himself in quiet trust. Was Judas in an impossible situation, a kind of pawn moved around in the great cosmic chess game, a sacrifice necessary before the winning move? Were the chief priests and Pilate inevitably going to respond in the way they did because it had all been foretold? If that is so then they cannot really be held responsible in the way that Matthew seems to lay responsibility on Jews. To be responsible implies freedom, but freedom implies that no one can determine beforehand absolutely the action that will be taken.

This is an old philosophical conundrum and, as it stands, it will remain problematic. It seems to me that Matthew was saying that human beings in their sin put Jesus to death but that God is able to bring triumph from tragedy, vindication for the just even in an unjust world. That is the Easter faith and the challenge is how do you live that out in what continues to look like a Good Friday world. We ought not to be too quick to apportion blame. We, too, are constrained by our prejudices, the expectations of our society, our own self-interest. What would we have done had we been in the crowd in Jerusalem? What should we be doing now?

A prayer

Living God, God with us, majestic in lowliness, powerful in weakness, we freely give ourselves to your saving purposes. Forgive us our sin, our jealousies and bitterness, our wrong compromises and foolish misjudgements. We ask that the power of your renewing, sustaining love may be in us, to teach, guide and grace our lives, through Jesus Christ our Lord. Amen.

Some questions and suggestions for further thought

1 What has struck you in your reading of Matthew's account of the crucifixion? Why are these features important for you?

2 Pilate washed his hands of Jesus. What reflections does this prompt in your mind?

3 Both Judas and Peter showed remorse at what they had done. What are the marks of true repentance?

4 Think about those events Matthew mentions at the death of Jesus. How would you give people today the sense that the cross is a 'cosmic' event?

4
Luke's story of the cross

Luke's Gospel is unique among the Gospels in at least two respects. First, it is the first part of a two-volume work: the Gospel and the Acts of the Apostles. Secondly, both are addressed directly to the same person, Theophilus. Theophilus is designated 'most excellent' which might suggest he is a Roman official of some rank.

Luke also tells us why he wrote as he did. He says that many others have compiled narratives of 'the things which have been accomplished among us'. All these Luke claims to have carefully examined but he now wishes 'to write an orderly account' that Theophilus may know the truth of the matter (1.1 – 4). That sounds as though some things that were being said needed correction and development. Perhaps charges were being laid which needed defusing and falsehoods which needed correcting.

As we know, Christianity started firmly within Judaism and only painfully and slowly became a different, distinguishable religion. The Romans knew the stubbornness of the Jewish people when it came to their religion. On a number of occasions they had tried to bludgeon the Jews into submission only to find themselves confronted by that extraordinary determination, and acceptance of martyrdom if necessary, which cannot be defeated when it grasps a whole nation. So the Jews continued to live in the Roman empire, treated with a grudging respect which the authorities seldom showed to others.

In the early days of the Church, when Christians were still keeping up their attendance at the temple and the synagogues, they were accorded the same protection that the Jews received. Quite probably, Rome did not distinguish between the two groups. However, as Christianity obviously became something more than a Jewish sect, so hostility came from both Jews and Gentiles. One of the ways in which racial and religious intolerance always shows itself is through false rumour and ridicule.

Moreover, in AD 64, Rome was set ablaze. Nero, needing scapegoats, blamed these new religious people called 'Christians'. So there was increased prejudice and persecution. Christians were watched by the authorities. Certainly the last thing the Church wanted to do was to draw unfavourable attention to itself. Christians increasingly needed to show how they sought only to live at peace with everyone.

Luke's Gospel was written later than Mark's, probably between AD 80 – 90. Luke writes to explain the Christian movement, to show its social virtues and to underline the fact that no one has need to fear its development or its gracious, compassionate leader. He wants to put to rest any fears that his fellow-Gentiles, or Roman masters, may have.

Luke writes primarily to give Christians an accurate resource as they try to walk the way of discipleship in an increasingly uncomfortable, social climate. He wants to encourage Christians by explaining the gospel and especially by recording what happened to people 'touched' by Jesus. Also he wants to defend Christians by explaining to the authorities just what the true nature of this movement is, what kind of a leader Jesus is, and what message he has for the world.

Luke was probably a Gentile, well-educated and a

clear-thinker. His Gospel suggests a lively social con-
science. He hardly touches on matters of Jewish
interest alone, but has his interest mainly fixed upon
the Gentiles and their world. He wants to build up the
Church in its faith through teaching and inspiration.
His desire is to commend the gospel to Jew and Gentile
alike, to give to those outside the Church a clear
account of what has taken place in the life, death and
resurrection of Jesus and an understanding of what is
happening, even how, in and through the lives of his
disciples.

The betrayal and the arrest   Luke 22.47 – 53

Obviously there are some differences between Mark's
account and that of Luke's. The crowd is mentioned
first, then Judas is identified. Luke does not mention
the crowd having weapons at this point, and so a
quieter, less hostile scene is suggested. Jesus is not
presented as the object of anyone's hatred, for the present at least.

Luke says that Judas drew near to kiss Jesus, but not
that the kiss actually happened. Later, a kiss was used
in Christian worship as a sign of love and peace. Did
Luke already find it hard even to think of Judas greeting
Jesus in this way? The omission of 'the kiss' spares
Jesus' dignity. In the same way Luke will later omit all
references to Jesus being bound.

Luke mentions 'those who were about him'. Are
these the disciples, those who stand in solidarity with
Jesus? They ask whether they should use their swords
(see 22.35 – 38) but, before there can be an answer,
violence takes place.

Jesus rejects all use of force, 'No more of this!'(verse
51). His hand reaches out and touches the slave, heal-

ing immediately the damage that has been done. This incident is only recorded by Luke.

The officers of the temple are said to come to arrest Jesus. This is another way by which Luke makes it clear that what is happening is not an ordinary arrest of an offender against the law. Jesus says that this is their hour and that of the power of darkness (verse 53). At the end of Luke's account of the temptation of Jesus (4.1 – 13) it is said that the devil left Jesus 'until an opportune time'. Luke sees the arrest and what follows as a struggle with satanic power. We note that there are no references to Scripture as being fulfilled, neither that the disciples forsook Jesus and fled.

Already some key Lucan themes are apparent, such as Jesus' moral stature, his dignity, his generosity and his compassion, even to enemies.

Peter's denial   Luke 22.54 – 62

Luke has a different order from Mark as well as changes in the content of the story. Jesus is brought to the high priest's house. There, during the night, Peter's denial takes place, and so does the abusing of the prisoner. Only when morning comes is Jesus brought before the Sanhedrin.

As Jesus is taken to the high priest's house, Peter 'followed at a distance'. Luke describes a courtyard scene with a central fire and people moving about to keep warm, in the half-light. Peter is part of the crowd and is accused by a maid in a general open way, 'This man also was with him.' The charge is tantamount to being a disciple and this Peter denies, saying, 'Woman, I do not know him.' At this point we should look back to 22.31 – 34 where Peter's denial is predicted. In particular, we should note the form of words used by

Jesus, 'I tell you, Peter, the cock will not crow this day, until you three times deny that you know me.' This is important because, as scholars point out, Peter's sin is not in denying that Jesus is the Christ, for that would be apostasy, but in denying that he knows Jesus by acquaintance, that he is a disciple. This is cowardice.

Another, a man this time, charges Peter with being 'one of them' and Peter denies Jesus a second time. Then, about an hour later, there is a further charge of discipleship and the denial, 'Man, I do not know what you are saying' and immediately the cock crows. Straightaway Jesus' word is fulfilled. Only Luke has it that the Lord turns and looks at Peter. Whereupon, Peter, remembering the Lord's words, goes out and weeps bitterly. These are repentant tears, part of his turning back (see 22.32).

Luke has emphasised Jesus' prophetic knowledge. Peter is here pictured as one who fails in courage, though not in faith that Jesus is the Messiah. Peter never joined those who made such a serious denial and clearly Luke does not expect his readers, Christian or otherwise, to defame Jesus. The call is to remember the word of the Lord and keep on following.

The mocking and the Sanhedrin   Luke 22.63 – 71

The mocking of Jesus by his captors takes place before the meeting of the Sanhedrin. In the Gospels of Matthew and Mark the 'sport' of the soldiers comes as a consequence of Jesus' Messianic claims. A cruel game of blindman's buff takes place as Jesus is tauntingly invited to use his special powers. There are no references to spitting, nor to the kind of allusions the other Gospel writers make to the songs of the suffering servant in Isaiah.

In the morning the Sanhedrin is called together – Luke describes them as the 'assembly of elders', language which his Greek-speaking readers would understand. Again, compared with Mark there are omissions – no false witnesses brought forward and no references to the temple for Luke's readers would have known that the temple in Jerusalem was destroyed by the Romans in AD 70.

The Council comes quickly to the question, 'If you are the Christ, tell us.' Jesus' answer challenges the spirit and purpose of the question. Will they believe his answer? Are they really sincere?

Verse 69 bursts upon the scene. In the other Gospels there are phrases like 'You shall see the Son of man coming . . .' and references to 'the clouds of heaven'. Luke has none of this imagery. Instead the affirmation is that 'from now on the Son of man shall be seated at the right hand of the power of God'. The earliest Christians lived with the conviction that the Lord would soon return in glory. As the years went by and life went on, Christians of Luke's generation realised that they might have a long haul ahead of them before the kingdom finally came. However, even in these present days, they believed, that the Son of man is the ascended Lord.

Luke says that 'all' ask whether Jesus is the Son of God and Jesus acknowledges the perception, the truth, in their question. They say they need no further testimony. Luke has no mention of blasphemy but those against him have clearly heard enough to bring Jesus before Pilate.

The trials before Pilate and Herod   Luke 23.1 – 25

Jesus is brought before Pilate and a formal threefold

accusation is made against him: perverting the nation, forbidding the payment of taxes to Caesar and claiming to be Christ, a king. It is noticeable, in the way Luke tells the story, that all these charges have a political edge to them. Jesus is accused of being an enemy of the Roman empire. It is also important to notice that, with Luke, it is not false witnesses who lay the charge against Jesus but the leaders of the Jewish people.

Pilate puts the central question, 'Are you the King of the Jews?' How is Jesus' answer to be read? Some scholars suggest as a question, throwing the challenge back to Pilate. Jesus could and would not deny his royal claims; however, the fundamental problem is that he and Pilate are using the same language but in different ways. Jesus is a king, but not in the sense Pilate means.

Pilate announces Jesus' innocence, the first of three such pronouncements. Luke is making it quite plain that this Roman governor does not see Jesus as a threat to Roman law and order. It is becoming increasingly apparent that the responsibility for what will happen to Jesus lies with his accusers, the chief priests and the multitude. They repeat their accusations that Jesus has stirred up the people as he has gone through Judea and Galilee, and now he is doing the same in Jerusalem.

Pilate seems to fasten on to the reference to Galilee. It was an unstable part of his domain, always threatening rebellion. But the mention of Galilee suggests that Jesus is a Galilean and therefore outside Pilate's jurisdiction. And, as it happens, Herod who is responsible to Rome for that part of the country is in Jerusalem. So Pilate – perhaps thankfully – hands Jesus on.

Herod receives Jesus gladly because, according to Luke (9.9), he has heard much about him and even hopes to witness a sign. Jesus remains silent during Herod's interrogation and the inquisitor gives up, doubtless in frustration. The chief priests and scribes vigorously repeat their accusation – Luke is again drawing attention to their attitudes. Herod sports with Jesus. There is a reference to the soldiers mocking and Jesus is returned to Pilate dressed in 'gorgeous apparel'. Herod also finds no fault in Jesus. Luke's comment about Herod and Pilate becoming friends may imply that they stand together against Jesus' accusers.

Now, back with Pilate, Luke brings the chief priests and rulers of the people on to the stage again. Pilate makes the second declaration of Jesus' innocence with regard to their charges and announces that Herod agrees with his judgement. Rome is saying that in no way is Jesus so guilty that he deserves the punishment of death. Pilate states his intention of scourging Jesus, to teach him a lesson, before letting him go.

Verse 17 does not occur in the best Greek manuscripts. Some scholars think it is a later insertion to make sense of what follows. Luke needs to explain that Barabbas is an insurrectionist and a murderer. It is the Jews who first mention him. He is their choice. Pilate keeps up his argument a little longer, speaking up for Jesus, but this only prompts stronger reactions as the crowd cries, 'Crucify!' Pilate again asks why, and makes the third affirmation that Jesus is innocent as charged. By now the crowd is all the more insistent in its demands and this crowd, like many crowds, is hard to resist. Their voices prevail.

Pilate's judgement is 'that their demand should be granted'. Luke is putting the responsibility for Jesus' death squarely on the shoulders of the Jewish leaders. No Romans are to blame, no soldiers abuse Jesus as it says in Mark and Matthew. Nor does Luke mention the scourging, for that would imply that a trial had taken place and judgement delivered according to Roman law.

Barabbas is released, the one who is the violent revolutionary, the known threat to society. Jesus is delivered up, handed over to the Jews. He becomes their responsibility.

So Luke emphasises in all this the innocence of Jesus, especially concerning the charges of insurrection and creating social disorder. The Romans themselves have found that the charges will not stick. Jesus was crucified for other than lawful reasons. The responsibility for this lies with the leaders of the Jews.

Simon of Cyrene and the women of Jerusalem
   Luke 23.26 – 31

Luke mentions Simon being pressed into carrying the cross. As in Matthew's Gospel, there is no mention of Alexander and Rufus, presumably because their names would mean nothing to Luke's readers. Luke says that Simon was conscripted and they 'laid on him the cross, to carry it behind Jesus'. (Look up 9.23 and 14.27.)

The verses about the women of Jerusalem (verses 27 – 31) are only found in Luke. He often mentions women in his story, much more than the other Gospel writers. These women set up loud wailings and lamentations as the procession makes its way to the place of crucifixion. Public mourning for a criminal is unlawful, so are these women acting in a courageous way, implicitly asserting Jesus' innocence?

Jesus speaks to the women. They are not to weep for him but for themselves in the light of what is to befall Jerusalem. Is this looking forward to AD 70 and the destruction of the city by the Romans?

Jesus says there are difficult, fearsome days coming when childless women will be glad. Barrenness was usually understood to be a disgrace for a Jewish woman, a tragedy in itself. Nevertheless, there will come a time when the suffering is so great that these women will be grateful that at least they do not have to see their children endure and suffer it. Hosea 10.8 is quoted in verse 30 with the implication that the coming terror is not some unfortunate accident of history but the judgement of God.

Verse 31 reads like a proverb and probably means here that if this is what happens to the innocent ('the green wood') what will it all be like for the guilty (the 'dry' wood)? These verses are a warning, a call even now to repentance.

Jesus is crucified with the criminals   Luke 23.32 – 43

With two criminals Jesus is led away to crucifixion. Luke uses this word 'criminal' – a word which some scholars think had a special, almost technical meaning after AD 70, and referred to Jewish Christians who took part in the armed revolt against Rome. Jesus is put to death with them.

Like the other Gospel writers, Luke simply says that 'they crucified him'. Jesus' prayer, 'Father, forgive them; for they know not what they do', is recorded only by Luke. The Greek wording gives the sense of the prayer being constantly repeated. Some later Greek manuscripts do not contain the petition, possibly because it was thought that God had not forgiven the Jews and that is why his severe judgement had fallen on Jerusalem in AD 70. But is it the Jews, or the crucifying soldiers, or the whole crowd for whom Jesus prayed? Whatever the answer the prayer is totally at one with the themes of forgiveness and mercy which Jesus preached and are shown in Luke's Gospel.

The soldiers cast lots for Jesus' clothes. He has often spoken of poverty. He dies possessing nothing.

Luke records the people watching, the rulers scoffing and the soldiers mocking. Again the temptation comes to Jesus to use personal power – 'if he is the Christ'. Jesus persists in quiet, obedient trust. The soldiers mock as they pour scorn on any would-be revolutionary. Yet Pilate's designation of Jesus reads very definitely, '**This is the King of the Jews**'.

The exchange between the criminals and Jesus is only recorded by Luke, who tells us they were 'hanged', using here the word found in Deuteronomy 21.23. One of the criminals reviles Jesus saying that he cannot save himself, let alone others. But, in the retort of the other (verses 40 – 41), we have clear Lucan theology. Is there no fear of God – we are under condemnation and justly in our case, but injustly in Jesus' case, for he has done nothing wrong? Jesus' solidarity with sinners is affirmed, but so is his innocence.

Also the criminal says, 'Jesus, remember me when you come into your kingdom.' Are these words a prayer of faith and hope, or is there a touch of irony? Jesus' response is the promise to him of Paradise today. Immediacy and emphasis on the present is a feature of Luke's Gospel (see 2.11; 4.21; 19.9). What is to come in the future is not denied in the present. The persistent criminal, who looks to the future for glory as did many first-century Christians, is assured that being 'with Jesus' today is to begin to know Paradise.

'Paradise', a Persian word, came to mean future bliss for the Jews, an equivalent term to 'heaven'. It was a relatively new development in Jewish thinking to teach

69

that at death the righteous go immediately to their reward. This idea seems to be used here, and also in the story of the rich man and Lazarus (16.19 – 31).

Again, Luke's interest in individuals, and in forgiveness and mercy for sinners, is apparent in this section.

Jesus breathes his last   Luke 23.44 – 49

In verse 44, Luke is following Mark's Gospel very closely. There is darkness until the ninth hour, 'while the sun's light failed'. Luke's word is *ekliponton*, our word 'eclipse'. The darkness at such an impossible time is a symbol of the awefulness of the moment. The theme of judgement is here.

Luke records that the temple curtain was torn before Jesus' final cry. Earlier in the Gospel, Jesus has affirmed that outcasts, traitors, sinners of all kinds will be first into the kingdom. He has just promised one of the criminals Paradise today. Now the temple curtain is torn, the way to God's presence is open and, following Jesus, the criminal will be the first to enter.

The great cry of dereliction is not recorded but, instead, Jesus commits his spirit into his Father's hands, using words from Psalm 31.5. The story of the crucifixion in Luke is bracketed with prayer: first, for the forgiveness of enemies, and lastly with trust in God. Prayer is a special emphasis in this Gospel and significantly Jesus, in his deepest anguish, prays for himself and his persecutors.

Jesus prays to his Father. Luke emphasises this relationship and in simple trust Jesus 'breathed his last'. Again, as with the other Gospel writers, Luke does not say Jesus dies. That would be too passive. He is giving himself even in death – especially, in death.

As we have followed Luke's story we have seen how both Pilate and the centurion state Jesus' innocence. This is in keeping with his apologetic purpose making it clear that the Romans have nothing to fear from the Christian movement since Jesus had no political pretensions at all. If Jesus was crucified as a political criminal, then such action was wrong. He was innocent of such charges; even Rome says so.

However, the centurion's statement says more. Luke tells us that the soldier 'praised God', presumably in recognition of what was really happening. And he declares Jesus not simply innocent but *dikaios* – 'righteous' (see Isaiah 53.11). There had developed in Judaism the understanding that the righteous are the poor, oppressed, persecuted people, despised by the wealthy and powerful who poured scorn on their faith in God. Luke is saying that Jesus died as one of these, the Christ of the poor, the oppressed, those who are discriminated against.

When the multitudes see what has taken place, they go home beating their breasts. This is a sign of repentance. Like the centurion who praises God, these also glimpse something of the deep, inner meaning of these events. They, too, have witnessed the divine action. An old order is giving way to the new.

Others also saw this. Luke mentions the 'acquaintances and the women', those who had followed, whose links with Jesus were never utterly broken.

Jesus is buried   Luke 23.50 – 56

Joseph of Arimathea is described as one 'looking for the kingdom of God'. He is pictured as a good, righteous Jew and a member of the Sanhedrin. Luke tells his readers that Joseph has not been party, nor given his consent, to the action against Jesus. He is one of a number of Jews, in Luke's Gospel, of special piety and perception – for example: Elizabeth and Zechariah (1.5 – 6); Simeon (2.25).

Joseph asks Pilate for the body of Jesus and takes responsibility for it. The body is laid in a new, rock-hewn tomb, on Friday, the day of preparation for the Sabbath.

The women follow all this, and see the tomb where the body is laid. Then they go to prepare the ointments and spices necessary for embalming. They can do no more than this because the Sabbath has come; but, at least, they are witnesses that Jesus is dead. They have seen the body and where it is laid.

Some special emphases

Luke seems to have written his books out of a mixture of pastoral, educational, evangelistic and apologetic intent. He has used Mark and other traditions. He wants to tell Theophilus and all his other readers what has happened. He keeps his historical purpose 'up front'; but there is no such thing as pure, recorded, uninterpreted history and Luke too has his special emphases. These are some of them:

✝ Luke sees a divine purpose being worked out in history and with the life, death and resurrection of Jesus a new and crucial step is taken in that purpose. What happens to Jesus must happen (22.22), but with that event a new age dawns. It is an age not confined to any place or time. It can show itself anywhere 'today' (23.43). It is an age that will be brought to completion in God's purpose but even now 'the Son of man shall be seated at the right hand of the power of God' (22.69).

✝ The coming of the new age is not without birth or death pains. From the beginning of his ministry Jesus found himself struggling with evil, as he was tempted by the devil. The struggle in the wilderness, in the garden of Gethsemane, and on the cross, as the crowd mocks and calls for a sign, are expressions of this struggle of cosmic significance. A result of Jesus fulfilling the Father's will, in trusting obedience, is that the message of God's love for everyone can now be proclaimed and lived in the whole world. It is for all people, Jew and Gentile. The new age, which struggled to birth in a world of religious and racial pain, now lives with a missionary birthmark indelibly impressed upon it.

✝ Luke certainly sees in Jesus' life of obedient faith, an example, a way for others to follow, even to death. In telling the story, Luke is already encouraging those who are struggling and persecuted in his day. Jesus is an example as he stands silent before his accusers (23.9), as he prays for forgiveness of his enemies (23.34), as he has compassion and as he brings hope to others (23.28,43). The way Jesus lived and died shapes the pattern for Christians and shows them how to bear witness to their faith.

✝ There can be no doubt about Luke's insistence on the innocence of Jesus. The Roman governor, Herod, the wailing women of Jerusalem, the criminal on the cross, the centurion at the foot of the cross, all declare that he has done nothing deserving of death. He is not a political trouble-maker, nor an ideological disturber of the peace. However, he does disturb people. They find themselves drawn into conflict with him, but this is the issue of truth against falsehood, and of God against sin. Jesus, and those who follow him, do not want to create anarchy, nor to set up their own political paradise. They live in the service of God and in trust of God.

So Luke affirms that Jesus is a righteous man, the innocent sufferer who goes the way appointed for him by God, even to death. He alone does not deserve death. He has done nothing wrong.

✝ In his death, and at other times in his life, Jesus directly associates himself with the outcasts, the despised, the marginalised, the handicapped and the criminals. This is even more than compassion. It is solidarity. He will be with them that they might be with him (23.43).

Thus we ought to note the special attention Luke gives to women, to Gentiles, and to the economically, socially and religiously poor. The Good News that this is the year of the Lord's favour (4.16 – 21) comes to all who are oppressed by others. Jesus dies with the criminals. He gives help to one of these, in his time of anguish, as he has often given himself to outsiders in his ministry. The signs of his victory, and of God's new age of salvation, come not with spectacular apocalyptic wonders, but with individual lives being changed, forgiveness received, hope shared and new beginnings made possible.

✝ Luke puts special emphasis on Jesus as a man of prayer. He tells of Jesus alone at prayer, of him calling on his Father in times of decision and tension. Therefore, on the cross, Jesus prays for his enemies, as well as in dedication to God.

✝ Finally, in Luke there is no specific indication that Jesus' death is 'for us' or 'a ransom for many'. The death of Jesus here is not the basis for the world's salvation – it is not atonement for sin. Jesus is 'one who serves' (22.27) and as such both Luke's first readers and modern believers can relate to him as the model of Christian piety. We are called to follow Jesus. Luke knows this is no easy discipleship and we shall come to recognise this point with Luke in the next section. What Luke is doing is giving the readers strong assurance that they have their place in God's salvation as they continue their witness as part of the world-wide church.

Some personal reflections

The first Christians looked for a swift and instant completion of all God's purposes in the 'coming again' of Jesus. By the time of Luke they realised that the coming of the kingdom may be some long time hence. Therefore, the Christian Church potentially faces many years of discipleship. The followers of Jesus must expect to take up their cross 'daily' (9.23).

Luke's Gospel has a realism about it. There are still victories to be fought and won in this present age. Just as Satan comes, not once, but again and again to tempt and distract Jesus, so the Christian community will find opposition, temptation and struggle to be their lot. Luke sees the 'present age' as a time in which the Church is called, in the power of the Holy Spirit, to witness to God's love in Christ. But one of the first stories of witness Luke tells is that of Stephen, dying in the name and manner of Christ (Acts 7.54 – 60). The Greek word for 'witness' is our English word *martyr*.

The 'little flock' are not to be afraid, however, because it is the Father's good pleasure to give them the kingdom (12.32, one of several injunctions in Luke about not being afraid). But for all that there is indeed Good News to be preached, announcing that God has visited to redeem his people (1.68) – there remains the real struggle with evil.

There is a way of talking about Christian living that suggests that it is all triumphant, glorious and powerfully straightforward. There is another way that sees it all as constant struggle. In fact, both perspectives need to be kept in tension.

Something of cosmic significance has happened in the life, death and resurrection of Jesus, and the Christian Church is called to bear witness to that. But the world will not easily acknowledge who is Lord, so the struggle of costly love will go on as new generations walk in the way of Jesus and affirm the kingdom. Both the reality of the work of God as Spirit and the reality of present evil threatening the world are taken together by Luke. An easy discipleship would not be understood by Luke but then neither would a joyless dutiful one.

We have seen how Luke asserted the innocence of Jesus so definitely. Moreover, this innocence was the pronouncement of the political authorities of the day. Formally, Jesus is not a threat to political order. But this does not mean that Christians should automatically become upholders of the *status quo*. There is an important sense in which Jesus is a subversive figure. He may not be primarily a political figure, if he is that at all, but his actions and teachings clearly have social and political repercussions. Anyone who comes announcing Good News for the poor, liberty for captives, and who can challenge accepted standards with regard to women, foreigners, and all kinds of discarded people, is going to be an irritant for those who are happy with the way things are.

All human societies create injustices. There are always marginalised, oppressed people in every nation. This does not mean that a formal policy of oppression is set in motion by those in power. It simply acknowledges that the social nature that is ours leads to various forms of injustice. Take the society in Britain as an example. There can be no doubt that racism is present in the common life. Some say it shows itself in the laws. It is certainly present in the churches and other social groups. There is anti-racist legislation which makes discrimination on the basis of colour illegal but, in subtle and less than subtle ways, it still goes on. People's attitudes are not changed just by passing laws. Many black people today experience feelings of being 'second class'. Another example of this is the presence of the long-term unemployed, particularly in the north of England. We find it hard to create a society in which this does not happen. Also, in far too many places, sexism rules and this is unacceptable.

The Jesus of Luke's Gospel seems to have had a special interest in, and relationship with, the marginalised people of his day. He was the friend of the discarded, the traitors and sinners. He praised the foreigner when the foreigner was worthy of praise and his attitude to women was remarkable for the day. Further, the Christian community which grew out of his teaching and preaching reflected something of his own spirit. So, although Luke can tell Theophilus and any other readers that this is not a revolutionary political movement, it clearly is subversive in that it challenges the values, attitudes and assumptions of its day in the name of the values, attitudes and assumptions of the kingdom of God.

The Church will always be this critical irritant in any society when it is true to its calling. Others may have what seems to them to be good reasons to pass by on the other side; but the kingdom of God is not like that. The Church, likewise, must be the Church for all the people of the world. The ancient division of Jew and Gentile, and any other old or modern divisions, have no place in this new humanity.

A prayer

O living God, of today and every day, whose love reaches out to every life and who would gather us all into your kingdom, save us from being petrified by our fears, forgive us our unworthy prejudices, and so fill us with your Spirit that the barriers between your children may be overcome in the power of your love and the joy of your kingdom which is coming and even now is among us. Amen.

Some questions and suggestions for further thought

1 What has struck you in your reading of Luke's account of the crucifixion? Why are these features important for you?

2 Luke is telling the authorities that as they had nothing to fear from Jesus so they have nothing to fear from the Church. Is this always the case?

3 Jesus identified himself with our humanity but the weaker, more vulnerable, discarded people seemed to have his special attention. What does this mean for the Church's calling?

4 'Father forgive them; for they know not what they do' (23.34). For whom is this prayer appropriate? Who can pray it? How will forgiveness be experienced?

5 'Today you will be with me in Paradise' (23.43). Discuss the significance of the hope of heaven.

5
John's story of the cross

'And now for something completely different!' – or so some have tried to say when referring to the Fourth Gospel. It **is** different from the Synoptics – Matthew, Mark and Luke – as reading of it will show. But it is not **completely** different, certainly not as much as some have hinted. After all, it is the same Jesus and the same crucifixion that the author recounts and proclaims.

Who the author is, when he wrote and to whom, are all questions that have produced something of a growth industry of scholarly answers. The authorship question, for example, is answered by some in the traditional way saying that he is John, son of Zebedee, the beloved disciple, while others suggest that the author is deliberately anonymous or that we are talking about a group of people who produced a number of editions leading to our present text! We are not going to summarise the results of this important industry. We shall call the author 'John' with the possible suggestion that some of what is written may well go back to the son of Zebedee but that others have remembered his teaching, added to it and developed it, so that our present Gospel is more of a corporate work.

What was the purpose of this Gospel? John's readers were basically Christians who had been part of the very remarkable spread of the Christian movement through the first century. This 'success' was not without its tensions and problems both within the Church and in the relationships between Christians and other citizens. John did not only write for the Church. He also had in mind those on the fringe and beyond its borders. For Christian and pagan he declared his purpose to be 'that you may believe that Jesus is the Christ, the Son of God, and that believing you may have life in his name' (20.31).

That is a very 'Christological' statement. Jesus is the Messiah, the Son of God. By believing, that is by trusting and obeying, the disciple enters into and receives life – 'eternal life' – is a favourite phrase of John. There is a clear stress in this Gospel on the humanity of Jesus and an equal stress on his divinity. Were there in John's experience those with 'faulty' Christologies? Many scholars think so. John is writing to emphasise this Christology in a context where some saw Jesus as less than divine and others saw him as less than human.

A traditional 'home' for this Gospel has been Ephesus. There seems to have been some hostility towards the Christian Church in this city, some of it coming from the synagogue. Ephesus was a Gentile, Greek city. It had a strong Jewish community (Acts 18.19) and also a continuing group of John the Baptist's disciples (Acts 19.1 – 7). John writes to proclaim the Gospel in this socially, religiously mixed culture, aware that some of those groups stand in opposition to Christ but convinced that all need to know of the one who is 'the way, and the truth, and the life' (John 14.6). He uses language that admits to several meanings. Perhaps he does this quite deliberately as he tries to address the message of the Gospel to Jew and Greek alike. Let us now look at John's story.

The betrayal and the arrest   John 18.1 – 12

John does not tell his readers the story of the agony of

Jesus in the garden of Gethsemane but he does report that it was a place where Jesus and his disciples often met, so it was well-known to Judas. He says that a band of soldiers with their officers come from the chief priests and Pharisees. It was the practice of the Romans to strengthen the temple garrison at festival occasions because these were potentially times of high tension and riot. John is underlining that Jesus' arrest is by religious **and** secular power. They came against the one whom John has identified as 'the light of the world' with their lanterns, torches and weapons.

John has already been very outspoken about Judas in his Gospel (6.70 – 71; 13.2,27), but here is no reference to the kiss because Jesus takes the initiative, steps forward and identifies himself. When they say they are looking for Jesus of Nazareth, he replies, 'I am he.' The statement may have a very deep significance. There have already been a number of 'I am' sayings in the Gospel, each one understood by John as a moment of revelation. Again, the Revealer speaks and John describes the response of the soldiers, the kind of response you would expect before God. Jesus is clearly above all earthly power, yet he gives himself to his captors.

Again they ask who he is and he identifies himself, adding only that his disciples be allowed to go in safety. (There is no reference to them forsaking him and fleeing.) John sees this concern for the well-being of the disciples as the fulfilment of Jesus' own words, probably 10.28 – 29. The theme of fulfilment, both of the Old Testament and of the words of Jesus, is important in John.

Only John mentions that it is Simon Peter who drew the sword and cut off Malchus' ear. There is no reference to Jesus healing the wound, but there is a stern command to put up the sword. Jesus asks, 'Shall I not drink the cup which the Father has given me?' John has not used the metaphor of 'the cup' before and seems to assume his readers will understand. Does it mean the eucharistic cup or is there an Old Testament theme here of the cup of God's wrath?

Before the high priest, and Peter's denial
John 18.13 – 27

Jesus was taken first to Annas. He had been high priest from AD 6 – 15 and was still a very influential figure. His son-in-law, Caiaphas, the high priest at the time, was a schemer, ready to make an unjust sacrifice if politically necessary (11.49 – 51).

Simon Peter, with another disciple, follows Jesus and his captors. Is this the beloved disciple who will run with Peter to the tomb on the resurrection morning? We are only told that he is known to the high priest and that he could use his influence to get Peter into the courtyard. There the maid makes her challenge: 'Are you not also one of this man's disciples?' And Peter denies the charge in the answer, 'I am not.' Perhaps we should see a contrast between Jesus' unambiguous, 'I am', and Peter's all-too-human falsehood.

Now the scene moves to Annas questioning Jesus. He asks Jesus about his disciples and his teaching. Jesus replies by reminding Annas of the openness of his ministry, in the temple and in synagogues. He has not tried to hide his work. Why doesn't Annas call witnesses? Asking for their testimony is the appropriate thing to do. At this point Jesus is struck by one of the officers, possibly for supposed insolence. It was an offence to abuse their rulers, including the high priest (Exodus 22.28).

Jesus is willing to have the witnesses called. He has nothing to hide. John's account makes it clear that the Jewish authorities are being unwarrantedly hostile.

Jesus is now sent, bound, to Caiaphas. Thus far there are no charges against him. Meanwhile Peter faces his second challenge and again denies that he is a disciple.

Then the question is put for the third time, from a relative of Malchus whom Peter wounded: 'Did I not see you in the garden with him?' There is no oath, no tears in this story. It is simply said that Peter again denies it, and at once the cock crows. The word of Jesus is fulfilled (13.38).

Jesus before Pilate   John 18.28 – 40; 19.1 – 16

Jesus is now brought from the high priest's house to the praetorium, the Roman procurator's official residence. Because this is the property of a Gentile, no Jew can enter it without becoming 'unclean'. The accusers of Jesus are more concerned, it seems, with religious ceremonial purity than moral justice and integrity. They wish to be clean so that they can eat the Passover, which implies that the last supper, in the Fourth Gospel, was not a Passover meal.

Pilate, whom John assumes is known to all for he has no introduction, comes out to the crowd and asks what is the accusation against Jesus. The reply is rather flat. Jesus is said to be an evildoer and that is why he is before the judge – hardly a specific charge.

Pilate counters with the suggestion that the Jews try Jesus by their own law, to which the significant reply is that they do not have the power of capital punishment. There is no elaboration of this comment but John sees theological significance in what is said in that another word of Jesus is being brought to fulfilment. Had he not spoken of being lifted up (3.14; 8.28; 12.32)? And was not the Roman way of death crucifixion? The Jews might stone a man to death. The Romans would lift him up on the cross.

The whole passage has its own vivid movement. Try to picture Pilate going into his court where Jesus is held. He puts the direct question, 'Are you the King of the Jews?' (This question is in identical form in all four Gospels.) It seems that this is the basic charge facing Jesus. Jesus puts his question in return. Is this Pilate's own question? Or is it the question of the Jews, or some others? The crucial matter here is what people understand by the word 'King'. How is Pilate understanding the words he uses?

Pilate abruptly turns the question aside. It is the Jews who have brought one of their own for trial. 'What have you done?' Pilate asks Jesus. Jesus keeps to the issue of kingship and acknowledges that he is a king but his kingdom is not of this world – that is, it does not have its origin and belonging here. His kingdom is not worldly and secular like Caesar's, but spiritual. That is why military actions to enforce its claims are utterly inappropriate.

'So you are a king?', asks Pilate. Jesus has confessed as much. He affirms his purpose in coming to this world. It is to bear witness to the truth. Those who live in the truth are those who recognise the rule of Jesus, they hear and obey his voice. Pilate asks, 'What is truth?' He still does not understand this strange man.

What he does understand is that Jesus is innocent and he goes outside to tell the Jews this. Jesus has committed no political offence, and no resistance was offered at his arrest. Then Pilate refers to the custom of releasing a prisoner of the people's choice at Passover. This custom is referred to in Matthew and Mark, but not in Luke. There is no evidence that it was a regular practice. He taunts them. 'Will you have me release for you the King of the Jews?' But the Jews will not have Jesus. They shout for Barabbas whom John describes as a robber, that is, someone who is guilty.

Jesus is scourged and mocked by the soldiers. He is crowned and dressed in purple. He is mocked **as a king**. The soldiers greet him with 'Hail, King of the Jews!' There is deep irony here.

Once more Pilate faces the Jews. He brings Jesus out to them because he can find no crime in him. Jesus appears, wearing the crown and the purple. 'Behold the man!' said Pilate, speaking more truly than he knew.

The chief priests and officers call for crucifixion. Pilate's reply has a sarcastic edge as he invites them to do what they cannot do, that is, crucify Jesus. Again Pilate says that Jesus is innocent. But the Jews insist that Jesus is not innocent according to their law, he has blasphemed in saying he is the Son of God and for that, he is guilty and deserves death (Leviticus 24.16).

John says that, when Pilate hears the claim that Jesus is the Son of God, he became even more afraid. (Remember how the Roman soldiers reacted in awe at the arrest.) Is this possible? For Pilate it seems it was certainly an awesome possibility that the Son of God should stand before him. The irony of the Fourth Gospel again shows itself. Who is really being judged here?

Pilate asks Jesus about his real origin but he receives no answer. At this Pilate tries to pull rank, assert his authority and let Jesus feel his judicial weight. Doesn't Jesus realise who it is that is questioning him? Jesus says that Pilate would have no power except it were given him from God. There is a stress in Jesus' words, Pilate would have **no** power.

John gives us the impression of a real battle going on in the mind of Pilate. He tries to release Jesus but this only provokes the crowd. They say that if Pilate lets Jesus go he is not Caesar's friend. This has the ring of hypocrisy about it because the Jews hated the Roman rule. They were not Caesar's friends but they are prepared to take his side against Jesus.

This stings Pilate and he comes out and sits at the place of judgement. This is a solemn moment and John gives the time, the date and the place, the sixth hour of the day of preparation for Passover at The Pavement. Jesus is brought forward and Pilate says to the Jews, 'Behold your King!' **Your** King, Pilate taunts the crowd. They respond with vehemence, they want to do away with Jesus, 'Crucify him!' Pilate presses the question, and we note again the irony, 'Shall I crucify your King?' An aweful moment follows as the chief priests utter the ultimate blasphemy, the final apostasy for a Jew, 'We have no king but Caesar.' It is not simply Jesus who is rejected here – they are saying that God (Yahweh) is no longer their King. They are no longer God's people – they have no king but Caesar. Jesus is handed over to them to be crucified.

The crucifixion   John 19.17 – 27

John omits a number of the details found in the Synoptic Gospels – for example, the taunting of Jesus, the darkness, the great cry of desolation. However, he has two additions: the dispute about the title on the cross, and the provision Jesus makes for his mother. Altogether the way John records the crucifixion has a less fraught, more serene quality about it, as Jesus is majestic in death.

The crowd take Jesus from Pilate. The Greek word is the same as that used in the prologue of the Gospel when it is said that, although the Word came to his own, his own 'received' him not (1.11). Now they 'receive' him only to reject him.

He goes to Golgotha carrying his own cross. The language is the same as that of Luke 14.27 which speaks of bearing the cross. No mention is made of Simon of Cyrene. Jesus alone carries the cross to the end.

John says simply that they crucified him between two others. There are no further details. Pilate has written the usual notice of the charge against the one condemned. It reads 'Jesus of Nazareth, the King of the Jews'. It was written in Hebrew, Latin and Greek so that Jews, Romans and Greeks should know the proclamation. Note again the irony of the Fourth Gospel. Jesus is the King, not of Israel alone, but for all the world. The chief priests protest. After all, Jesus only claimed to be King of the Jews. But, for whatever reason, Pilate insists on what he has written. Once more he unwittingly proclaims the truth.

Four soldiers make up the crucifixion detail. It was their right by custom to share out the victims' possessions. Jesus' tunic is made of one piece so they gamble for it and, as John says, the Scriptures are fulfilled. Like the Synoptics he sees what is happening as the will of God.

Standing around the cross were Jesus' mother (whom John never names), some other women and the 'the disciple whom he loved'. This figure is never formally identified. Tradition has it that it is John, son of

Zebedee. Jesus entrusts his mother to his care. She loses one son and gains another son. A new relationship is begun at the death of Jesus between his mother and one who knew the mind of her son. Even in death Jesus has compassion and looks to the future for those he must leave (16.7).

Jesus gives up his spirit   John 19.28 – 30

The keyword in these verses is the word 'finished'. The sense in which John uses it here is of completedness or accomplishment. There is a note of achievement, perhaps also of triumph.

The beatings, the strain, the cross, all have tired Jesus and he is thirsty. John shows quite clearly the humanity of Jesus. Just as people cry in bereavement (11.35), are troubled at some daunting task (12.27), and are thirsty (19.28), so is Jesus. John does not dwell on the horror of crucifixion, but he has no doubt that Jesus, in all humanity, really hung and suffered there.

He also sees this cry as fulfilling Scripture, not that Jesus suddenly thought of the text and cried out, but that all that is appointed in Scripture for Jesus is brought to an end.

His last word from the cross is one word in Greek – 'Finished!' All that had been given him to do is now summed up in the finality of this moment. Nothing more is to be done. He has loved to the end. He bows his head and gives up his spirit. No one, even now, takes his life from him, he offers it up, offering himself, totally to God. It is his free act. The Son has done the Father's will until there is nothing more to do – 'Finished!'

Jesus is taken from the cross and buried
John 19.31 – 42

In all three Synoptic Gospels the death of Jesus is followed by some word of great significance and proclamation. The centurion says, 'This man was the Son of God' or 'Truly this man was innocent'. John has no such reference. He does not 'need' a Gentile or anyone to declare a truth which in the Fourth Gospel has been affirmed from the beginning. But he does have a comment to make and he does it using a story.

According to John's chronology Jesus is crucified on the day of preparation for the Passover, which is also the Preparation for the Sabbath. Perhaps he is not so much concerned about the date and time as making a theological point. According to Jewish law it was necessary that Jesus, and the others crucified with him, should die quickly so that their bodies could be removed from the cross before nightfall. So the request is made to Pilate that the crucifieds' legs be broken since this is a recognised way of hastening their death. Therefore, the two crucified with Jesus have their legs shattered. But, when the soldiers come to Jesus, they find that he is already dead, so his bones are not broken.

What a soldier does is to stab open his side, probably to certify death. John says that from this wound there flows blood and water. He, the author, bears testimony to this happening and he tells the readers so that they may believe with confidence. He believes that this happened to fulfil the Scripture. The reference to no bones being broken probably relates to Exodus 12.46 and the issue of water and blood to Zechariah 12.10. But what does all this mean?

It is hard to say with certainty. Some scholars suggest that here we have an example of the 'hidden sacramentalism' of John's Gospel. The 'hiddenness' is in the fact that John nowhere describes either the baptism of Jesus or the Last Supper. But such an interpretation is not convincing.

A closer attention to the texts suggests another possibility. The reference in Exodus about not breaking bones refers to the Passover lambs. Is John, therefore, affirming that Jesus is the true Passover lamb, with no broken bones, the Lamb of God who takes away the sin of the world? This is a less than accurate suggestion because the Passover lamb was not killed for the forgiveness of sins. The text from Zechariah (12.10) in verse 37 is a prophecy that God will pour out his spirit on Israel and the inhabitants of Jerusalem so that when they look on the one they have pierced they shall grieve and mourn as for an only child. Is John affirming that the Jews will come to mourn the 'piercing', the killing of Jesus when the spirit comes?

Joseph of Arimathea takes Jesus' body for burial. He is said to be a secret disciple, for fear of the Jews. Were there others in that situation among John's readers? Nicodemus, who first came to Jesus by night – in the dark and therefore not a disciple, 3.2 – now associates himself with him, bringing spices for the burial. The amount mentioned is enormous, such as might be used for a king. John is aware of the haste necessary. The body is wrapped in linen cloths with the spices and laid in a new tomb. John again tells us this was the day of Preparation. But preparation for what?

Some special emphases

John's account of the passion is at the same time like and unlike the accounts in the Synoptics. There are particular emphases of his, present through the whole

Gospel, that are expressed in the story of the cross. Here are some of them:

✝ In 19.9 Pilate is pictured as asking Jesus where he has come from. What is his origin? Where does he belong? It is a question that, in various forms, arises again and again in the Fourth Gospel. There is a specialness about Jesus. He is clearly and unambiguously a man, suffering the pains and emotions we all feel. The Word has really become flesh. Jesus is 'pleased as man with man to dwell'. But he has come 'from above'. His is the special relationship of Father and Son, so that whoever sees the Son sees the Father. No wonder then that Pilate and the soldiers fall back with fear and awe before him.

✝ Jesus is a majestic figure in John's account of the cross. The fulfilment theme we have seen in the Synoptics is repeated but there is a more vivid sense that the initiative is with Jesus. He goes out to meet events. Judas has no opportunity to indicate the one he has come to betray, Jesus steps forward and announces himself. He is the one in control. He has a task to complete and he moves steadily on until it is finished.

✝ In this sense we have to ask who is being judged. Jesus stands before Pilate, the man of worldly power and authority. Jesus is his prisoner. But who is really the judge? Judgement is an important theme in the Fourth Gospel. It is not primarily Jesus' task to judge people, certainly he did not come to condemn. But he comes as the light of the world and one of the inevitable effects of light is to reveal darkness. The light shows up the darkness and what is hidden in the darkness. Pilate is Jesus' judge but as we read the story we realise, by the very manner and response of Jesus, that something more is going on. Jesus can make Pilate tremble. Pilate brings no fear to Jesus.

Pilate comes across as sympathetic to Jesus. He pronounces Jesus' innocence and does not appear in any way to be dismissive of him. By contrast John paints the Jewish authorities as hostile. In the Fourth Gospel there seems to be an emphasis on symbolic figures. Both high priests, Annas and Caiaphas, are mentioned and, along with other Jewish leaders, they want the death of Jesus. They are ready to commit apostasy. If John was a Jew by upbringing, like Matthew, perhaps he is working out his sorrow and anger at his own people. Perhaps also the Christians of John's day were themselves being hassled by the Jews and put out of the synagogues (16.2 – 3). The Fourth Gospel certainly reflects some hard feelings against God's ancient people.

✝ The way Jesus speaks up for his disciples at the time of his arrest and the particular care he expressed for his mother are in keeping with the special concern shown by Jesus to those who were his friends and disciples. This would be very reassuring for John's church.

✝ The royal character of Jesus is something to which we have already drawn attention. We do so again to emphasise the stress on the phrase 'King of the Jews'. John underlines this in the discussion between Jesus and Pilate on being a king, in the charge eventually brought by the chief priests and in the placard hammered on to the cross for all the world to see and read. The Fourth Gospel does not dwell like the Synoptics on the phrase 'The kingdom of God', but there is no doubt who is set forth as King.

✝ In the way John tells the story it is not Jesus and his disciples who draw back but the soldiers and the imperial governor. John omits the mocking, the taunting, the darkness, the cry of dereliction because the King is accomplishing his royal task. The Son of God goes to the cross unperturbed in the strength of the Father's promise (12.28). So the cross is to be seen as accomplishment and exaltation. Jesus is lifted up to death and glory; and, in the obedience of the Son, the Father is glorified. The passion is the way back to heaven. There is more stress on this aspect than on suffering, although there is no underplaying of the reality of the crucifixion of Jesus.

✝ The whole gospel is an act of love. It is because God so loved the world that the Son was sent with a task to accomplish. The love is expressed in the refusal to condemn, in the refusal to utter any words of judgement and retaliation, in the care for a mother, and in the total dedication to the divine purpose of salvation. Later, seeing the wounds of love, and the man of the cross raised to life, Thomas is to say, in the climax of the gospel, 'My Lord and my God!' (20.28).

Some personal reflections

It may come as a surprise to some readers to learn that, when the final list of those books which make up our New Testament was being completed, John's Gospel was not an automatic choice for inclusion. Centuries later, many wonder how this could have been so since this Gospel has been such a source of strength, comfort and inspiration to so many. But the fact is that some early Christians had doubts about it. Why?

One of the reasons was that its language and theology were considered dangerous. John's world was a world of many religions, some with secret language and ceremonies. What John seems to have done is to tell the story of Jesus in language which was both 'at home' in Jewish thought and in that of Greek philosophies and religion. So it was open to various interpretations, or dangerous misinterpretations as some thought. Certainly some less-than-Christian groups used and quoted John's Gospel approvingly, or at least those parts and phrases of it that fitted their philosophies.

In running the risk he did John showed himself to be an evangelist. He wanted to tell the story of what God had accomplished in and through his Son so that people should believe on the One sent by the Father and, in believing, know eternal life. An evangelist has a basic story to tell but she or he is mindful of the audience, speaking in words and ways that will get the truth across without unnecessary hurdles to jump. John had that preacher's desire and so he was bold in his choice of words.

Undoubtedly, at times, what he has written is ambiguous in meaning. We tend to judge ambiguity as a weakness – we want the meanings to be clear, sharp and definite. 'Why can't he say what he means?' we exclaim about those whose arguments we have found it hard to follow, whose meaning we do not instantly understand. Now, some people's ideas are hard to follow because they themselves are muddled in their thought and presentation. Their message is not clear primarily because it is not clear in their own mind. But there are others who are not instantly clear because what they are saying is so deep that it is difficult to put into words. They struggle, they are selective in their words, looking for analogies and appropriate metaphors. They are ready to take risks to get it across.

Sometimes, therefore, ambiguity is deliberate. For

example, when John speaks of Jesus being 'lifted up' he intentionally means the phrase to have a double meaning. Jesus is 'lifted up' **both** on to the cross **and** to glory. 'Being lifted up' means both these at the same time.

In John's Gospel there is the recognition that events can be understood at different levels. They have more than one obvious meaning. Living on the surface, just glancing at what you think is happening, may cause you to miss what is really going on. For some, what happened at Golgotha was the crucifixion of three trouble-makers. So it might appear to a visitor in Jerusalem. He would return home after the Passover and tell his friends that he saw three men cruelly killed in the Roman way. He would have seen, yet not seen. There may be a hiddenness in events, as there is a hiddenness in language, especially language about God. Perhaps that is one of the reasons why Jesus promised the Holy Spirit to his disciples to help them call to mind all he had said and done, and lead them into all truth (14.16,26; 16.13). We can be given the same Spirit to enable us to discern what God is doing in the events of our time. By that same Spirit our faith and trust may be renewed through new perceptions of meaning in the story of the cross.

One feature of John's account which we noticed was the discussion of kingship. Jesus is King, but what kind of King? What kind of leadership does he offer? What is the true nature of his authority? This debate goes on in the Church, involving issues of political involvement, secular power, status and influence. What is the relationship of the kingdom of Christ to the kingdoms of this world? When hearing Jesus say, 'My kingdom is not of this world', it is tempting to follow an unworldly highly spiritualised form of discipleship, ignoring the political and social aspects of our existence. But if that is the message and the form of love, why ever did God become incarnate? Why did the Word become **flesh**? These are immense questions and they have been debated and discussed by the Church through the generations. The Jesus of the Fourth Gospel washed the disciples' feet, stood before Pilate and died as one caught in a political machine, yet majestic in it all. What is the nature of the kingship of God, his authority and power, not just in our personal existence but in the totality of the universe?

Lastly among these reflections, Jesus' final word from the cross was 'Finished!' We have noted that this is not a word of despair and exhaustion, but of completedness and accomplishment. But what actually is finished?

Christians have often interpreted the life, death and resurrection of Jesus as having cosmic consequence. A great battle was fought and won, once and for all. Evil and death are defeated in the glorious victory of Christ the Lord. But, we are painfully aware that this still looks all too much like a Good Friday world. Jesus may have died proclaiming, 'It is finished', but the next morning Pilate went about his business, the high priests continued their less than glorious ministry, the Zealots plotted revolution and the vast majority of the human race found life exactly the same as before.

However, the first Christians knew as painfully as we do the reality of sin within them and around them. If it was appropriate to speak of Jesus winning a victory it was also clear that there are still struggles ahead until all God's purposes for creation were accomplished, and finished.

But, for all this struggle, what made and kept them – and perhaps us – Christian, was the conviction that in the life and death of Jesus they had glimpsed something of the heart of God, of a love that will not let them go. What was finished was the work the Father had given the Son to do – it was a work of revelation, of light in darkness, of loving to the end. He loved and loved until there was no more life to give. Many of us are thankful beyond words that this Jesus has gripped our lives, that the love which is fundamental, real and abiding, has broken through our blindness and dullness.

Love, so amazing, so divine . . .
See from his head, his hands, his feet,
 Sorrow and love flow mingled down.

Isaac Watts

Has anyone seen anything like this, any love like this? The heart of God's undying love for the world is exposed. That is what is finished. It remains for ever the most important news to hear and believe.

A prayer

Living God, invisible to our eyes, yet seen in your Son Jesus Christ, we praise you that you so loved the world as to take our humanity and, in your Son, bear our pain and die our death. May your light ever shine in our darkness, your truth be our way, your finished work our hope and your service our joy. We thank you that in Jesus we have glimpsed grace and truth and, in your mercy, received eternal life. Amen.

Some questions and suggestions for further thought

1 What has struck you in your reading of John's account of the crucifixion? Why are these features important for you?

2 The Jewish leaders seemed to value religious ceremony above justice and human need. What is it about religion that can make it so dangerous?

3 Are military actions always inappropriate in terms of God's kingdom?

4 Political pressures and religious prejudices combined to crucify Jesus. Where in the world today can you see these forces at work? Is there any way to learn about the victims? How can we help them?

5 Imagine you are talking with someone who is not a Christian believer. Tell them how you understand that Jesus' work is finished and that that is good news.

6
Telling the story of the cross today

It is not my purpose in this last chapter to try and gather up all the various thoughts that have been expressed and shape them into one final conclusive comment. I shall not try to do that fundamentally because I do not think it can be done! What I do want to attempt to do is to reflect on the story with regard to our discipleship and witness today. The cross is central to Christian life. Arising from our reading of the four Gospel accounts, what are some of the implications for us today?

In the first chapter I argued that, although the four gospels tell the same story, they do not tell it in an identical way. That point I hope, has been well-illustrated. We have seen how each has different emphases, varied details and, to some extent, distinguishable theologies. These differences are not to be overstated but neither are they to be ignored. The variety is there partly because of the contexts out of which these Gospels came but that is not the only reason for the various insights and emphases. The work of the Holy Spirit in calling the story of Jesus to the minds of the disciples is not to be overlooked!

However, I want to underline, in particular, two implications of this, because of what they mean for Christian living today:

First, it is significant that, from the beginning, there emerged acknowledged but different ways of telling the story of Jesus. It means that there never was one final, definite way of understanding and proclaiming the cross of Jesus.

Mark and John were both Gospel writers but they did not see Jesus in the same way, nor did they understand his message in identical terms. Matthew and Luke likewise had different understandings – one appreciating the Jewishness of Jesus, the other emphasising Jesus' response to Gentiles. Some of the Gospel writers drew heavily on Old Testament themes to interpret Jesus and his cross, while others were less committed to these images and saw the significance of Christ's death in different terms.

But why should anyone expect all Christians to see and speak the truth in the same way? Too often the Church has been over-anxious about this diversity of experience and doctrine, perhaps because of a fear that the diversity will be too far-spreading and some will 'go overboard'. That has happened, as some interpretations of Jesus have looked more like their originator's reflections, than the Jesus of the Gospels. But that should not lead us to the other extreme of a monochrome single view to which all must subscribe or else be adjudged wrong.

This diversity of perception of the one Christ in the New Testament is not a weakness, but a strength. Let us be thankful that God has given us what he has through the insights and limitations of his messengers: Matthew, Mark, Luke and John.

Christians can welcome this diversity. It comes, if we believe in the inspiration of Scripture, from the Holy Spirit. The four Gospel writers had different perceptions, but one Lord. An important contribution Christians could make in our contemporary and divided society is to show how we can have different opinions and perspectives within a common loyalty. Do we all have to believe exactly the same in order to be Christians? Is that what Christian believing means? This is not an argument for an openness in which 'anything goes'. Rather, it is a recognition that diversity is a feature of our inheritance from the New Testament, a diversity for which we can give thanks to God.

The second implication relates to the suggestion that the background and situation of the Gospel writers have helped to shape their understanding and presentation of the gospel. One illustration of this point, easily overlooked is that the New Testament itself is written in 'common' Greek, not the Aramaic that was spoken in Galilee. The gospel message was not just for Galilee, and so translation was necessary from the first if the message was to be got across.

There is a two-way influence between the background and situation, and the Gospel. The way the gospel story was told, and indeed what was included and excluded, relates to its background and situation. That is shown in the differences between Mark and John. But the Gospel also had its influence on its situation, causing people to see familiar things in a new light. That is why Christians were said to have 'turned the world upside down' (Acts 17.6).

The Church must always be aware of the people, the ideas, the pressures and influences among which it lives, and then be able to speak the Good News appropriately to that situation. When I described the three different churches in the first chapter I tried to show that, as living Christian communities, they attempted to respond to their own needs and situation in creative ways. I can remember the gratitude many of us felt when J. B. Phillips' translation of the New Testament became available. It was in our language, speaking as part of our situation. That translation reads in a rather 'dated' way now, and there are better alternatives for today, but it served a generation and more.

I have specially mentioned translations but the point also includes the question of content. Mark mentions Alexander and Rufus to his readers because their names would presumably mean something. The other Gospel writers do not mention the sons of Simon of Cyrene. They add nothing to the story. Now, that is a very small detail, so let us fasten on to a more controversial point. All of the Gospels, in varying degree, place the responsibility for the death of Jesus on the Jews. Some hard things are said and the consequences through the centuries have been enormous. Some Gentile, Christian children have been taught that the Jews were 'God-murderers'. The Gospels have been used at times to support a wretched anti-Semitism.

Much of modern historical scholarship inclines to the view that Jesus was crucified for political reasons more than anything else. Perhaps we have to understand that the situation out of which the Gospels came was one where Judaism was hostile to Christianity and there was mutual bitterness which led to a less than complete telling of the story. The situation of the writers had its effect. This is not to say that chief priests, elders, scribes and Pharisees were not responsible for Jesus' death, only that to lay all the blame on them is unjust. The 'anti-Jewish polemic' of the Gospels has led to some terrible results in history. The situation has had its effect but it is not creative in this instance.

What remains true about the cross, in every historical situation, is its power to touch and transform lives. Christians believe that here something of abiding significance is revealed. Sometimes that truth has been of comfort, for the cross speaks of the infinite love of God. Here is an absoluteness of suffering and sacrifice

– that 'greater love'. At other times the word of the cross has been disturbing as it stands in contradiction to so many of our human values and assumptions. If it declares the truth about God, it also reveals something of the truth about ourselves. It raises questions about our compromises, our blindness, our willingness to resort to violence, and our loyalty.

Can we say that we would have done anything but contribute to the cross if we had been there, either by fleeing, denying or being indifferent? Yet, it is the thought of God that comes through most strongly, that in some sense this is the Lord's doing and it is marvellous. As they tell the story, Christians interpret the meaning of the cross. All kinds of images have been employed, of victory, of service, of the lawcourt, the slave-market and more. All have tried to communicate the amazing affirmation that this is God's cross, for us. So the cross speaks of hope in our despair. It is no easy hope, like cheap optimism; but it is costly, like all love. Above all, it is costly to God.

How can your church share the message of the cross today? What will you be doing next Good Friday in your situation? What I am hoping for from this book is that you and I, and the congregations to which we belong, will look again at the stories of the cross with our eyes, ears and minds wide open to what is happening around us now. I pray that we shall **hear** the message of the cross for our world today. That has happened in generations past and the Church and society have been renewed by the 'hearing of the word'.

Therefore, I shall conclude with four more of those brief **personal reflections** in the hope that you will be prompted to record what you see is the message of Christ's cross for our world.

First, the cross is for those who know what it is like

for their life to fall apart. We cannot get inside the mind of Jesus, of course, but we have heard the great cry, 'My God, my God, why have you forsaken me?' He had staked all on the doing of the Father's will. He had spoken of God's kingdom, present and to come. But the cross is cruel in its pain and even more in the sense of total abandonment. Where is God? What is happening? Why have you forsaken me?

This is the cry from the pit of despair. It is the point of breakdown, of darkest depression, when all sense, hope and meaning are gone, dreams become nightmares and memories only come to mock. It is the place where one's whole sense of worth and purpose is painfully pinned down by a vast question mark. It is a fearsome, frightening place. Jesus has been there.

His experience of this despair is unique, because no one has ever known the Father as Jesus did. But there are those who have gone into their own dark valleys, who have seen before them the gaping darkness with its hollow laughter echoing in unfathomable depths. They know the weight of depression.

This can happen at all ages and in such different circumstances – failed examinations, broken engagements, personal moral failure, bereavement, redundancy. I have known people in all these circumstances who find their faith shaken and their experience of life to be that of forsakenness. Why me? Why anybody? Where are you, God? 'I pray,' said one woman, 'but the ceiling sends my words back to wound me.'

There is no easy answer to this agonising experience. But this we can say – Jesus has been there. He knows what it is to feel forsaken and to be forsaken. His experience was real and painful; but we also know that this was not his last experience. If this is not true, then how can this dark aspect of our human life ever be redeemed? In Isaiah 53.3 we read:

'He was despised and rejected by men;
   a man of sorrows, and acquainted with grief.'

Good Friday reflections might help some to become aware of who it is that is with them in their present agony. Perhaps, with help, we will be able to probe a little deeper into the dark mystery of the cross, and find hope and comfort in our situations of despair.

Secondly, the cross happened because there were those who wrongly identified their tradition with the truth. The story of Jesus entering Jerusalem and weeping over the city contains a sharp phrase in the *New English Bible*: 'because you did not recognise God's moment when it came' (Luke 19.44). It is a tragic scene. In the city were those who believed in God, took their religion seriously, prayed for the Messiah to come but, because they thought they already knew what the Messiah would be like, called for the crucifixion of this one who did not keep to their tradition.

We must not be quick to judge. The prophets had been stoned before Jesus, and since. The Church has sometimes been fearfully deaf and blind to what God is saying and doing and all too often truth is sacrificed in the name of tradition. This is not done by wicked people. Often they are 'pillars' – faithful and loyal. Their tragedy is one of limited vision. They do not know what they are doing. 'Lord, if we had seen you hungry, or thirsty, or naked, or in prison . . . or on the cross . . . we would have been the first to help.' But we do not 'see', sometimes because of that wilful blindness and fear called prejudice. We see some aspect of the truth and falsely imagine it to be the whole. It is an understandable temptation but its consequences are wounding and destructive.

I can illustrate this from my own experience. I think of: a man who confessed to homosexual feelings, although he never practised them, was asked to leave his church; a young couple, glad of their new faith, wishing to be married in church but were turned away by three different ministers because the woman had been divorced; a man who spoke of the agony of either being patronised or ignored because he was black; a student who was made to feel a traitor and faithless because he dared to share his doubt at a Bible study.

Jesus did not come to condemn the world. Condemning is easy; but saving the world is something else. 'Father, forgive them, for they know not what they do' (Luke 23.34). That is Christ's prayer for us all, in the Church and outside. It is for all of us who completely identify our tradition with the truth, and fail to be open to new understandings and revelations of God.

Thirdly, the cross happened because of political expediency – 'It is expedient . . . that one man should die for the people,' said Caiaphas (John 11.50; 18.14). Pilate, fearing the loss of public order, washed his hands to appease a restless mob. Jesus was the victim of powerful men in dangerous circumstances.

We ought not to be too quick to blame. Much of our political life requires careful judgement and compromise. We have ideals and in a perfect world these dreams would be fulfilled. But we live in the real world where calculated risks must be taken and not everything is possible. Some will get hurt. Life is like that.

I now live in one of the large towns of Northern England and cannot help but be aware of high unemployment and other social distress. No one should minimise what a personal and spiritual tragedy this is for so many people. Rightly or wrongly, so much of our self-identity is linked to our work. Have you noticed how an early question we put to a new acquaintance is 'What do you do?' According to the answer we unconsciously categorise or value the person. So we can imagine the pain that this innocent enquiry brings to some people and why they go to such lengths to avoid an answer.

This wastage of so many people is tragic. It has come about for several reasons but undoubtedly one of them is the values which have found expression in political policies. The great enemy, it was said, was inflation, and the price of success in the struggle to win the victory over that included a high level of unemployment. It was said to be expedient. No one deliberately wanted it that way but political choices were made and the inevitable social consequences followed.

Suppose, however, that the values you wanted to defend were not the most important. Suppose that choice were wrong. Suppose there were worse enemies than inflation. Then, was the price worth it? The question is important because it drives us back to basic matters of worth and value. Both Caiaphas and Pilate feared an uprising fuelled by religious zeal – with good reason! But there might be worse things to fear.

We must pray for our politicians and others in positions of power and responsibility. They have a fearful task. There was a cruel kind of sense in the decisions of Pilate and the chief priests; but they made the wrong choice. Perhaps we have to admit that all our choices are at best ambiguous. Only one man made all the right responses, living perfectly in the will of God – and look what happened to him!

The cross stands in judgment on all our social theories and ideologies. Politicians and other leaders are only poor sinners, like the rest of us, struggling to do their best for the common good. The cross has a word for them which is both critical and creative. Good Friday is a day to pray for ourselves and our leaders, that we might make the right decisions.

Fourthly, the cross is the place of wonder. The evangelists all record, in their different ways, the fact that this death had immediate effect. The soldiers and the governor fell back before Jesus. The centurion at the cross confessed that this was the Son of God.

Christian thinkers have filled many books with theories about the cross, writing their theologies of atonement. They have tried to express in words what it all means as sacrifice, liberation, victory and love unlimited. Many great and abiding insights have been given to us through their work. But the deeper power of the cross is in the way it evokes worship. It is the place where standing, looking, and paying attention is most appropriate. Who is here? What is happening? The theories attempt to answer these questions, but those who 'see' find themselves at worship. The inexpressible is here. What is revealed, or better still, 'who' is revealed, is beyond words. Good Friday is a day to watch, and pray, to wait and wonder, and to worship.

The cross is not, of course, the end of the story. Friday comes and it is dark but Sunday is already on its way. God has and will have the last and final word. We must not forget this lest our religion becomes a stoical following of a noble martyr, all duty and no joy, all suffering and no hope. Cross and resurrection belong together, for both are the action of God. We have paused in this book at the cross of Jesus. It remains a strange and challenging story. A bored generation can be at once frightened and fascinated by One who staked all on God. Or is it the story of God who staked all on us? It appears as foolishness, an absurdity in our reasoning world, a sign of contradiction. But the heart of the Good News is Christ crucified. There may be different ways of recounting and understanding this old story but it goes on being told because here is the power, the wisdom and the love of God.

A prayer

Living God, who in your Son suffered our sin, bore our pain and died our death, grant us grace, that before the cross we may, by your Spirit, behold your love, receive your forgiveness, know your peace, and praise your glory. We worship, we adore, Father, Son and Holy Spirit. Amen.